Anonymous

A brief History of the Church of Jesus Christ of Latter-day Saints

From the Birth of the Prophet Joseph Smith to the present Time

Anonymous

A brief History of the Church of Jesus Christ of Latter-day Saints
From the Birth of the Prophet Joseph Smith to the present Time

ISBN/EAN: 9783337162207

Printed in Europe, USA, Canada, Australia, Japan

Cover: Foto ©Lupo / pixelio.de

More available books at **www.hansebooks.com**

A BRIEF HISTORY

OF THE

CHURCH OF JESUS CHRIST

—OF—

LATTER-DAY SAINTS,

FROM THE BIRTH OF THE PROPHET JOSEPH SMITH
TO THE PRESENT TIME.

BY THE AUTHOR OF THE "LIFE OF BRIGHAM YOUNG."

"And in the days of these kings shall the God of heaven set up a kingdom, which shall never be destroyed: and the kingdom shall not be left to other people, but it shall break in pieces and consume all these kingdoms, and it shall stand forever."—*Daniel* 2: 44.

SALT LAKE CITY, UTAH:
GEO. Q. CANNON & SONS CO., PUBLISHERS.
1893.

PREFACE.

The following pages contain a brief history of th · Church of Jesus Christ of Latter-day Saints.

In order that the reader may obtain a clear understanding of the principles of the gospel, in connection with the history of the people who have been instrumental in establishing it, references have been made freely to the Book of Doctrine and Covenants containing the revelations of the Prophet Joseph Smith for the building up of the Kingdom of God in the last days.

In conjunction with his own experience, the author has gathered his facts, in sketching these main outlines of the faith, work, travels and persecutions of the Saints, from a large number of reliable authorities on the subject. Accuracy has been aimed at, as well as completeness as far as the limited space would allow.

The volume is designed, first, to create an interest in the marvelous work of God, as exemplified in and through the Mormons, in the minds of the youth of Israel, to whom a knowledge of the faith, toils and sacrifices of the founders of this great, latter-day religious fabric is absolutely indispensable. Secondly, there is a large class of persons who desire a glimpse of the story of Mormonism, but who have no time to read the more ponderous books thereon; such, it is believed, will find ust what they need in these pages.

THE AUTHOR.

September, 1893.

CONTENTS.

I. FROM THE PROPHET'S BIRTH TO THE ORGANIZATION OF THE CHURCH.

1805–1830

"A MARVELOUS WORK AND A WONDER."	9
MESSAGE FROM ON HIGH	15
THE SACRED HILL CUMORAH	21
TRANSLATING THE RECORDS	25
IMPORTANT REVELATIONS	30

II. FROM THE ORGANIZATION TO THE FLIGHT FROM KIRTLAND.

1830–1838

ORGANIZATION OF THE CHURCH	35
MANIFESTATIONS AND PERSECUTIONS	37
MISSION TO THE LAMANITES	43
THE LAW OF CONSECRATION	52
LOCATING THE LAND OF ZION	54
PROGRESS IN KIRTLAND AND THE EAST	58
EXPULSION FROM JACKSON COUNTY	62
HIGH COUNCIL ORGANIZED	66
ZION'S CAMP	68
APOSTLES AND SEVENTIES CHOSEN	71
DEPARTURE FROM CLAY COUNTY	75

III. FROM THE MISSOURI EXODUS TO THE MARTYRDOM.
1838-1844

BANISHED FROM MISSOURI	89
LOWERING CLOUDS	96
THE MARTYRDOM	100

IV. THE CHURCH UNDER BRIGHAM YOUNG.
1844-1877

AGREEMENT TO LEAVE NAUVOO	105
EXPELLED FROM ILLINOIS	109
TWO MILITARY PICTURES	113
THE PIONEERS AND THE FIRST COMPANIES	117
MIGRATION OF THE MAIN BODY WEST	122
COLONIZATION	127
UTAH TERRITORY ORGANIZED	131
EVENTS FROM 1854 TO 1857	139
THE UTAH EXPEDITION	142
A PERIOD OF RECUPERATION	149
OFFICIAL CRUSADE—DEATH OF PRESIDENT YOUNG	164

FROM THE DEATH OF PRESIDENT YOUNG TO THE PRESENT TIME.
1877-1893

JOHN TAYLOR CHOSEN LEADER	160
THE EDMUNDS-TUCKER AGITATION	163
CHANGED CONDITIONS	165
THE TEMPLES OF THE SAINTS	168
CONCLUSION	172

A BRIEF HISTORY OF THE CHURCH.

I. FROM THE PROPHET'S BIRTH TO ITS ORGANIZATION.
1805—1830.

1. "A MARVELOUS WORK AND A WONDER."

WITH the age of reason, or freedom in religion, that followed the flight of Luther from the debauched court of Pope Leo X, came also the age of skepticism—not alone skepticism, but hypocrisy, while the revolution in theology, inaugurated by the reformers, shattered the thought-monopoly which had been concentrated in the Pope; it likewise created such diversities of opinion, and so many leaders in religion that the world of mankind were literally "children tossed to and fro, and carried about with every wind of doctrine, by the slight of men and cunning craftiness, whereby they lie in wait to deceive."

There was no universally acknowledged head of the Christian Church. It is true that since the death or martyrdom of the Apostles of Christ, God had acknowledged no authority on the earth. All had apostatized from the true gospel, and the Apostles, Prophets, Evangelists, Pastors and Teachers, which Christ had acknowledged or commissioned, were no more to be found; the Christian Bishops had departed from the simple ordinances of the Christian religion, and instead had introduced Jewish and Pagan observances, ceremonies and mysteries, for the purpose of gaining friends. But for centuries all Christians—often through compulsion,* however,—had acknowledged the pope as the vicegerent of God, and had recognized his authority. But the sweep of the reformation broke this power over men. Following Luther, Zwingli, Calvin and Cranmer, arose a hundred leaders in religion, who, disregarding the injunction, "And no man taketh this honor unto himself, but he that is called of God, as was Aaron," set themselves up as officers in the Church of Christ. The reformation broke the power of popedom, and gave to men the blessed right of private judgment; but, going one step further, the Protestants, like the Catholics, from whom they had emancipated themselves, usurped authority, for nowhere is there a record, nor even a profession made, that authority was conferred, by revelation from God or the ministration of angels the only known methods by which it could be done, upon anyone to act in His name.*

This disregard of authority brought with it a train of many evils, chief among which were hypocrisy, and a service of form instead of a worship from the heart. So continued the condition of the people almost three hundred years, from the reformation to the beginning of the nineteenth century.

The Prophet Isaiah foresaw this period, and declared

---

* It is said that Roger Williams refused to continue as pastor over the largest Baptist Church in this country, because there was "no regularly constituted Church on earth, nor any person authorized to administer any Church ordinance; nor can there be, until new Apostles are sent by the Great Head of the Church for whose coming I am seeking." See "Picturesque America," page 502.

of the people of the earth, at this time: "Wherefore the Lord said, forasmuch as this people draw near me with their mouth, and their lips do honor me, but have removed their heart far from me, and their fear toward me is taught by the precept of men: Therefore, behold, I will proceed to do a marvelous work among this people, even a marvelous work and a wonder: for the wisdom of their wise men shall perish, and the understanding of their prudent men shall be hid."*

This "marvelous work and a wonder" which the Lord was to accomplish, was the restoration of His authority unto men, and the establishment and organization of His authorized Church upon the earth, as predicted anciently by the Prophet Daniel, and by John the Revelator:

"As for thee, O king, thy thoughts came into thy mind upon thy bed, what should come to pass hereafter: and he that revealeth secrets maketh known to thee what shall come to pass.   *   *   *   And in the days of these kings shall the God of heaven set up a kingdom, which shall never be destroyed; and the kingdom shall not be left to other people, but it shall break in pieces and consume all these kingdoms, and it shall stand forever.†"

"And I saw another angel fly in the midst of heaven, having the everlasting Gospel to preach to them that dwell on the earth, and to every nation, and kindred, and tongue, and people, saying with a loud voice, Fear God, and give glory to him: for the hour of his judg-

---

* Isaiah, xxix, 13, 14.
† Daniel, ii, 29, 44.

ment is come: and worship him that made heaven, and earth, and the sea, and the fountains of waters."*

The words of John the Revelator explain how the Gospel was to be restored. It was to be done in the same way that God adopted in ancient times, as recorded in the holy scriptures, by the visitation of angels, and by revelation. Save through these channels, how could Jehovah make known His will to men? As in the days of the Apostles, so in modern times—the household of God was to be "built upon the foundation of Apostles and Prophets, Jesus Christ himself being the chief corner stone." Its officers were to be in possession of the gifts and of "the spirit of wisdom and revelation."

In the midst of all the uncertainty and chaos of opinion, God was to reveal Himself, and out of conflict establish peace, out of disorder, union and oneness of purpose, so that, as formerly, there might be "One Lord one faith, one baptism, one God and Father of all," etc.

The beginning of this "marvelous work" was inaugurated in the dawn of the nineteenth century, when God revealed Himself personally, and by the visitation of angels, to the Prophet Joseph Smith, and chose him to be the leader of the dispensation of the fullness of times, and to be the instrument to introduce the gospel of Christ by authority, to establish and organize the true Church of God in the latter days.

Through that Prophet was brought forth the wonderful record called the Book of Mormon—a book which contains a fullness of the gospel as taught by our beloved Savior. Thirty editions of this work have been printed — many thousands of volumes — and scattered

---

* Revelation, xiv, 6, 7.

broadcast to the English speaking world, while its precious truths have been read by thousands in each of the eleven foreign languages into which the book has been translated.

The Church of Jesus Christ of Latter-day Saints was organized on the 6th day of April 1830, in the town of Fayette, Seneca County, New York. It is built upon the rock of revelation, and through this means, its officers have received authority from God to act in their callings and enjoy the gifts and powers of the gospel as was the case with the ancient Apostles. Its mission is one of peace; its aims and objects, the preparation of the people for the second coming of Christ, the inauguration of the Millennium, and the establishment of the universal brotherhood of man.

"But we do not believe this claim, it is visionary, impossible!" say some of the readers. "It cannot be possible that this is the 'marvelous work' spoken of and foreseen by the ancient seer."

In reply, it must be said that such is the claim of the Latter-day Saints, or the Mormons, as they are erroneously called. If they are justly entitled to it, their history for the past sixty years should partially demonstrate the fact. Their doctrines speak for themselves.

Who shall deny that the Saints are entitled to the claim they make when a review is taken of the record of the accomplishments of this strange people?

From forty members, in 1830, the following of the Church today has grown to hundreds of thousands. Then it had the Prophet Joseph alone to declare its doctrines, now it has missionaries in all liberal nations of the earth. It has prospered through the fire of severest persecution. Driven, peeled and scattered, their Prophet and Patriarch basely murdered for their testimonies, its members have rallied with each onslaught, and pressed on with the work with greater force and power than before. It counts its martyrs by the score, its heroes and heroines by the thousands. Driven from their homes in Illinois, they were marvelously sustained by God in their wonderful exodus to the Rocky Mountains. In this wilderness of the West the rich blessings of the Lord have followed them in the establishment of one of the most prosperous, thrifty and happy commonwealths of our nation. To it have been gathered tens of thousands of the poor from the nations of the earth to build up and beautify the latter-day Zion, virtually fulfilling the prediction: "And many people shall go and say, Come ye, and let us go up to the mountain of the Lord, to the House of the God of Jacob; and he will teach us of his ways, and we will walk in his paths: for out of Zion shall go forth the law, and the word of the Lord from Jerusalem."* And this one: "The wilderness and the solitary place shall be glad for them; and the desert shall rejoice and blossom as the rose."†

Temples, schools, houses of worship, cities and villages have sprung up in the thirsty wilderness, and the result of the thrift and labor of this peculiar people may be seen in their beautiful homes, gardens, fields, herds, and possessions in the whole region of the great West: while the religious truths promulgated by them without money or pay are taking root, yea bearing fruit, not alone in their own midst but in every Christian land. Having discarded dead forms, the members of this Church

---

* Isaiah, ii, 3.
† Ibid, xxxv, 1.

worship from the heart and point to a living faith, fully sustained by noble works. Their Church organization is unsurpassed, the government unequaled in modern annals. They build temples for the worship of God and for the performance of ordinances for the living and the dead, and the path of their persecutions, as well as the land which they now peacefully inhabit, is dotted by these holy structures. Everything about them points to the peculiar people that were to be established in the latter days, their whole career is a "marvelous work and a wonder."

2. Message from on High.

Joseph Smith, the Mormon Prophet, and the founder of the Church of Jesus Christ of Latter-day Saints, was born in Sharon, Windsor County, Vermont, on the 23rd day of December, 1805. When the lad was ten years of age, his parents, Joseph Smith, Sen., and Lucy, his wife, removed from Vermont to Palmyra, Ontario, now Wayne, County, New York. Four years later the family moved into Manchester in the same county. The elder Smith was an honest farmer, with humble surroundings, in straitened financial circumstances, having lost much of his property through the treachery of a trusted friend. He had seven sons and three daughters, of whom Joseph, the Prophet, was the fourth child.

At this period, Western New York was a new country in most respects; Ohio and Illinois were yet a wilderness, and beyond Missouri, which was then the limit of the United States, lay the practically unexplored regions of the wild Indian tribes.

The inhabitants of the frontier region of the great

Empire State were poor, plain in their living and dress, generally religious, or spiritually inclined, read the Bible, went to church, and lived in all respects, excepting the religious, much like the pioneer of the great West—a familiar character now fast disappearing from our land has continued to live up to the present day. There was doubtless more religion, as it is called, in the life of the early frontiersman than in that of the later pioneer of the West. Sixty years ago, the various and conflicting sects went enthusiastically wild in their camp meetings and revivals—much of which excitement has died out by the promulgation of common-sense religious views since then. About two years after the Smith family's removal to Manchester, there was a great religious revival in the district thereabout. Multitudes united themselves to the numerous creeds, and when there were no further proselytes to make, priests and converts turned upon each other to contend concerning principles and dogmas, until excessive confusion and bad feeling prevailed.

Members of the Smith family were divided, some joining one society and others another. Young Joseph inclined to the Methodists, but his mind was in a state of uneasiness owing to the disunion which existed. For this cause, he kept himself aloof from all parties, "awaiting the hour when the divine message should stir the waters of his soul." In the midst of the surrounding tumult, he often said to himself: "What is to be done? Which of all these parties is right? Or, are they all wrong together? If any of them be right, which is it, and how shall I know it?"

In this frame of mind, he was one day reading the Epistle of James, the first chapter and fifth verse: "If any of you lack wisdom, let him ask of God, that giveth to all men liberally, and upbraideth not; and it shall be given him." Here was new inspiration; he had never thought of his condition in this light before. Certainly God, the Father of religion, could impart the truth. The youth determined to enquire of that unfailing source, and so on a beautiful morning, in the spring of 1820, he retired to a sylvan glade in the woods to call upon the name of God. Finding himself alone, he bended his knees, vocally for the first time offering up to his Maker the desires of his heart. Then a mysterious power of darkness overcame him: he could not speak; his soul was filled with a horror presaging instant destruction. He felt himself in the fell grasp of an unseen personage of darkness. His soul went up in unuttered prayer for deliverance, and as he was about despairing, the gloom rolled away, he saw a pillar of light descending from heaven, and approaching him. The darkness fled with the enemy that had afflicted him. As the light fell upon the prostrate lad, he saw two personages, in the form of men, glorious above description, standing above him in the air. One of them calling him by name spoke, saying:

"This is my beloved Son, hear him."

Gaining control of his thoughts, he remembered the object of his search, and enquired which of all the sects was right. In answer he was told that none of them was right, and that he must join none of them. Said the glorious Being: "They draw near to me with their lips, but their hearts are far from me; they teach for doctrine the commandments of men, having a form o Godliness, but they deny the power thereof." Joseph was amazed at the instruction, for up to this time it had not entered his mind that the true church was not to be found upon the face of the earth. Repeating their command that he should not ally himself with any of the man-made sects, the personages withdrew, the light vanished, and the youth recovering, found himself lying on his back gazing up into heaven.

Repeating the wonderful vision of what he had seen and heard, it created wide surprise, not to say consternation and amazement. He was accounted a blasphemer for announcing that the Father was a personage, and still worse, that he, an obscure boy, had seen Him and the Son, and had heard their eternal voice. His parents and his brethren believed, but not so the professors of religion. One of the ministers to whom he confided his vision told him flatly that it was of the devil. There were no such things as visions and revelations in these days. Such manifestations had ceased with the Apostles, and there would never be any more. But the lad remained true to his trust, and as a result he was persecuted, stigmatized as a dreamer, a knave and a hypocrite. His life was sought, he was persecuted and slandered, but still he said: "I had seen a vision. I knew it, and I knew that God knew it, and I could not deny it, neither dare I do it; at least I knew that by so doing I would offend God and come under condemnation." Thus nothing could change the steadfastness of his testimony which he maintained through the toil, poverty, scorn and tribulation of the following three years, during which time, forced from the society of his former friends, he was obliged to seek the companionship which his genial and social nature craved among those unnoted for their goodness, among evil characters, as he himself confesses. Thus he fell frequently into many foolish errors, and he felt greatly condemned at times for his weakness and imperfections.

He was at length forced to seek the Lord that he might receive a forgiveness for all his sins and foibles, and know his standing before his God. On the night of September 21st, 1823, he prayed earnestly for an answer to his petition, and while thus engaged the darkness began to fade away, and a glory appeared, until the room was lighter than noonday. In the midst of this light, in the air by his bedside, stood a radiant personage, whose countenance was lovely and more bright than vivid lightning. Calling the youth by name, he declared himself a messenger from God whose name was Moroni. He said that the Lord had a work for Joseph to do—that through him God's power and kingdom were to be restored to earth, and that his name should be had for good and evil among all nations.

He was shown in vision the hill wherein were hidden the gold plates containing the record of the Book of Mormon, and with them the Urim and Thummim, prepared by the Almighty to aid in the translation of the book. The angel then quoted from the scriptures various prophecies relating to the restoration of the gospel and the Priesthood, and the setting up of the Savior's latter-day kingdom and the ushering in of the Millennium. He referred to the prophecies included in the fourth and part of the third chapters of Malachi, the eleventh chapter of Isaiah, the twenty-second and twenty-third verses of the third chapter of Acts, and the last five verses of the second chapter of Joel, saying these were about to be fulfilled. He declared that the "fullness of the Gentiles" would soon come in, and warned the youth that when he should obtain possession of the plates of the Book of Mormon he should not show them to any one except by commandment of God, otherwise he would be destroyed. The angel then left, the room grew dark save just around the ascending messenger, who disappeared by way of what seemed a conduit right up into heaven.

Powerful emotions crowded upon the mind of Joseph as he lay musing on the scene, marveling upon the things which had been revealed to him. While he yet pondered, the angel made his second apperance, standing in a blazing glory to repeat the solemn message to the listening youth. He related word for word what had been said before, adding that great judgments, desolation, famine, sword and pestilence were coming upon the earth. Again Moroni ascended, shortly thereafter returning a third time, repeating all that had been said before, and adding by way of caution, that Joseph must not give way to a mercenary spirit which would tempt him, owing to his poverty, to secure the plates for purposes of gain. The heavenly ambassador then disappeared as the twilight in the east heralded the approach of day.

Having thus spent the night in holy communion with the angel, Joseph left his bed at his usual hour of arising, and proceeded to his daily toil on the farm, but he was unable to work. His father bade him return to rest in their home. On his way his strength failed him, and he fell helpless to the ground as he was crossing a fence. A voice aroused him by gently speaking his name. He looked up and saw once more beside him the angel of the previous night. For the fourth time he related the heavenly message to the future prophet, closing with a command that Joseph tell his father of the visits, the commandments received, and of what he had learned of the purposes of God. He obeyed, and standing there in the field, he related to his father all that had passed. "My son, these things are of God; take heed that you proceed in all holiness to do His will," said the elder Joseph when his son had finished his narration.

3. THE SACRED HILL CUMORAH.

On the road from Palmyra to Manchester, about three or four miles from the former place (twenty-five miles south-west of Rochester, New York) is situated the hill Cumorah. Its north end rises abruptly from a plain to the height of about 150 feet. It is the highest of the many hills in the neighborhood, and is locally known by the name of "Mormon Hill."

It was to this elevation, named Cumorah by the ancient Nephites and Ramah by the Jaredites, that Joseph, the Prophet, proceeded, just after obtaining his father's consent and blessing, on the eventful morning referred to in the previous chapter. He knew the place immediately from the vision he had seen of it. He relates that "on the west side of the hill, not far from the top, under a stone of considerable size, lay the plates deposited in a stone box; this stone was thick and rounding in the middle on the upper side, and thinner towards the edges, so that the middle part of it was visible above the ground, but the edges all around were covered with earth." Obtaining a lever, he raised the stone, looked in, and there indeed beheld the plates, the Urim and Thummim, and the breast-plate as stated by the messenger. "The box in which they lay," he continues, "was formed by placing stones together in some kind of cement. In the bottom of the box were laid two stones cross-ways of the box, and on these stones lay the plates and the other things with them."

Stretching forth his hands to remove the contents, Joseph was immediately restrained by the messenger, Moroni, who told him that the time had not yet arrived, but that four years must elapse before the records should be delivered into his hands. He was instructed to repair to the sacred spot each succeeding year on that day, where the angel would meet and instruct him in what manner the Kingdom of God was to be conducted in the latter days. The messenger cautioned him to prove faithful, in the meantime, and likewise imparted many precious truths to the youth: telling him, among other things, that he, Moroni, while living on the earth four centuries after Christ, had hidden the plates in the hill; that he was the last of a line of prophets who ministered to an ancient people, called Nephites, who inhabited this land; that he was the son of Mormon, a Nephite prophet, general and historian, whose record the plates contained.

Having finished his instructions and ended his counsel, the angel disappeared, and Joseph, carefully covering the box and replacing the soil, returned to his home, where he related his experience, confiding to the members of the household all that he had been empowered to reveal. They believed in his wondrous story, and rejoiced in the knowledge that God had spoken from the heavens.

Each succeeding 22nd day of September, the hill Cumorah was visited by Joseph, each time he met and communed with the heavenly messenger, each time gazed upon the precious records, each time received instructions that expanded his intellect and gave him a more perfect conception of the marvelous work which God was about to found.

The period which now followed, when he was between the ages of eighteen and twenty-two years, was to be the most important in his life for the shaping of his character. It was a probation. In it he passed through the preparatory course in which the Lord fitted the future prophet for the responsibilities incident to the establishment of His Church upon the earth which should endure forevermore.

Joseph toiled diligently upon his father's farm until his younger brothers were able to attend to the duties there and at home. Then, at the age of twenty, he sought employment at a distance. His engagement carried him to Harmony, Sesquehanna County, Pennsylvania, where he was employed by a Mr. Josiah Stoal, of New York, in digging for a silver mine which his employer imagined existed in that region. The mine was a failure, and Joseph, who was greatly respected by his employer, prevailed upon the latter to abandon the undertaking, which was accordingly done. While thus employed, Joseph boarded at the home of Mr. Isaac Hale, with whose daughter Emma, he became enamored. His love was reciprocated, but the parents, being prejudiced against the youth by the stories of his enemies, circulated to injure him because he still continued to assert that he had seen a vision, would not for a time consent to their union. Under these circumstances, the girl being of age, high-minded and devout, they acted without consent, and were married in South Bainbridge, Chenango County, New York, by Squire Tarbill, on the 18th day of January, 1827. Returning with his wife to his father's home in Manchester, he assisted in the labor on the farm to obtain means for his family and his mission.

Upon these two incidents—his being employed to dig for silver and his marriage away from his wife's father's home—were based the accusations of his enemies that he was a "money-digger" and "wife-stealer."

The end of his four years' probation was rapidly approaching. Joseph had been faithful to his trust. Not once had he failed in his prescribed visits to the sacred hill. Faithfully had he kept the counsels of his heavenly teacher. In his preparatory work, he had been sincerely supported by his wife and his brethren, who participated in his hopes and did much to comfort his heart in the midst of the assaults and ridicule that were heaped upon him.

At length the promised day arrived; for the fifth time the youth stood upon the spot where the sacred records were concealed. It was the morning of the 22nd day of September, 1827. With a prayer that he might prove faithful to his trust, he removed the cover of the box, and, stretching forth his hands at the angel's command, took from their hiding place the treasures there safely hidden for fourteen centuries. Lifting them to the surface, he examined their beauty.* Then it was that the

---

* "The Urim and Thummim was two precious stones set in an arch of silver, which was fastened to an ancient breast-plate of pure gold, curiously wrought. The breast-plate was concave on one side and convex on the other, and seemed to have been made for a man of greater stature than is ordinary in modern days. Four golden bands were fastened to it, for the purpose of attaching it to the person of its wearer—two of the bands being for the shoulders, the other two for the waist or hips.

"The plates, also of gold, were of uniform size; each was slightly less in

angel charged him to shield the records from profane sight and touch, to guard them as sacredly as he would his life. He was now alone responsible. If, through any neglect, he should suffer them carelessly to be destroyed or to go, great should be his chastisement, and he should finally be cut off, but, if he should use all care to preserve them until they should be called for again by the messenger, they should be protected from the efforts that would be made to rob him of them, and he should have the support of heaven and come off triumphant.

"Moroni disappeared, and the Prophet of the Last Dispensation stood alone upon Cumorah, clasping to his bosom priceless trust."

4. TRANSLATING THE RECORDS.

Soon it became apparent why Joseph had been cautioned by the angel to guard the plates so carefully. No sooner had he begun his homeward journey than he was assaulted by evil persons who sought his destruction. Three times, on the short journey to his home, he was attacked by unknown men who endeavored to strike him and rob him of his charge. Once he was hit with a bludgeon. However, he reached home with the plates unharmed, though himself bruised and weakened from the

---

thickness than a common sheet of tin and was about eight inches in width and all were bound together by three rings, running through one edge of the plates. Thus secured, they formed a book about six inches in thickness. A part of the volume, about one-third, was sealed; the other leaves Joseph turned with his hand. They were covered on both sides with strange characters, small and beautifully engraved."—Cannon's "Life of Joseph Smith." p. 49.

contest. But the persecution was continued, falsehoods were cunningly set afloat concerning him, prejudice walled him in, assassins lurked by his pathway seeking his life, mobs surrounded his home, every means was adopted by his enemies for his destruction and to gain possession of the plates. But while all their efforts in these directions failed, his enemies succeeded by these means in preventing Joseph from proceeding with his work of translation, and the persecution at length became so unbearable that he was forced to flee from Manchester. He then determined to go to the residence of his wife's father in Pennsylvania.

No sooner had he decided upon this course than poverty, another seemingly insurmountable barrier, presented itself; but this was relieved by the timely aid rendered by a Mr. Martin Harris, a respectable and well-to-do farmer of Palmyra Township, New York, a friend who was inspired to assist the Prophet in the midst of his afflictions with a gift of fifty dollars. By this means he was enabled to reach his destination in Pennsylvania. Twice on this journey, Joseph was stopped by officers, armed with pretended law warrants, who searched the wagon in quest of the golden plates, but again they were unsuccessful.

Early in December, 1827, he reached the residence of Mr. Isaac Hale, his father-in-law, where he was kindly received, the anger of his wife's parents over the young people's independent action in getting married having evidently abated.

Immediately after his arrival, he began copying the characters of the plates, and by means of the Urim and Thummim translated some of them, in which labor he was engaged from the time of his arrival to the following February. It was some time during this month that his friend Martin Harris visited him to learn more of his wondrous mission. Soon after, Mr. Harris carried away to New York some of the copies and translations made from the plates, the object being to show them to some scientist or linguist who should determine on their genuineness; for while Mr. Harris believed, he was evidently not without his doubts.

Being shown the characters, Prof. Charles Anthon, of Columbia College, stated, according to the account of Mr. Harris, that the translation was correct, more so than any he had before seen translated from the Egyptian. The Professor was then shown the untranslated characters, which he said were true Egyptian, Chaldaic, Assyric, and Arabic. He gave a certificate, addressed to the people of Palmyra, embodying the expressed assertions, and gave it to Mr. Harris, who folded it, placed it in his pocket, and was about to leave, when the Professor enquired how the young man learned that there were gold plates in the place where he found them.

"An angel of God revealed it to him," was the farmer's reply.

"Let me see that certificate," said the astonished Professor. Mr. Harris complied, thinking the learned man desired to add something to it, but no sooner was the paper in the Professor's hands than he tore it in pieces, saying:

"There is no such thing in these days as ministering of angels;" adding that he wished the plates brought to him, and he would translate them.

"A part of the plates is sealed, and I am forbidden to bring them," said Mr. Harris, whereupon the Professor contemptuously replied:

"I cannot read a sealed book."

And thus were fulfilled literally the words of the ancient Prophet of God, as written in Isaiah xxix, 11.

Dr. Mitchell, another learned scholar, was consulted, and seconded all that Prof. Anthon had said concerning the characters and the translation. The related incident converted Mr. Harris to the testimony of Joseph, and, returning, he offered to become the scribe of the Prophet in the work of translation, which proffer was gladly accepted. Their joint labors in this work continued from April 12th to June 15th, 1828, by which time 116 pages of manuscript had been translated, and was copied by Mr. Harris.* At this time, the latter much desired to show his wife and other skeptics these pages, and at length, much against the will of Joseph, received permission to do so, on condition that only certain persons named should be allowed to see the writings. This pledge was broken, and the manuscript was stolen, being never again seen by Joseph, who thus angered the Almighty, and besides lost his gift of translation for a time. Mr. Harris, though he was forgiven, and afterwards became one of the Three Witnesses of the Book of Mormon, never again acted as Joseph's scribe. Joseph's wife now assisted him for a short period in the work of translation, but owing to her household duties,

---

*The following is the manner in which it is said the Book of Mormon was translated: "The Prophet, scanning through the Urim and Thummim the golden pages, would see appear, in lieu of the strange characters engraved thereon, their equivalent in English words. These he would repeat, and the scribe, separated from him by a veil or curtain, would write them down. * * * Until the writing was correct in every particular, the words last given would remain before the eyes of the translator, and not disappear. But on the necessary correction being made, they would immediately pass away and be succeeded by others."

and the loss of their first-born, in the summer of 1828, slow and tedious progress was made.

Joseph prayed earnestly to the Lord that he might receive assistance in the task before him, and in answer to his petitions there came to his door, in Harmony, a young school teacher, named Oliver Cowdery, who had heard of and believed in the angelic vision of the Prophet. He offered his services as scribe and secretary, which were eagerly accepted, and the hindered work again proceeded on the 7th day of April, 1829, advancing so rapidly that by the middle of the following May its greater part was completed.

While the work progressed, not only were many precious truths revealed from heaven to the young men, but from the records themselves they gleaned many glorious principles that gave them great joy. But persecution continued unabated, so much so that if Joseph's father-in-law had not given them protection it is doubtful that they could have proceeded. Timely financial aid was rendered them by Joseph Knight of Colesville, Broome County, and at the residence of the Whitmer family, friends of Oliver Cowdery, at Fayette, Seneca County, they found a home in which the latter portion of the records was translated, they having been invited to come there by David Whitmer.

At length the translation was completed, the plates were re-committed into the charge of the angel Moroni, who received them back into his keeping until the time shall come when the unsealed portions are to be brought forth.

The Prophet and his friends visited at Palmyra Mr. Martin Harris to arrange for the publication of the work for which that gentleman was to furnish the money. Arrangements were made with Mr. Egbert B. Grandin to print 5000 copies for three thousand dollars, and the copyright was secured on the 11th day of June, 1829. While Joseph visited his home in Pennsylvania, during the autumn of 1829 and the succeeding winter, Oliver Cowdery remained to give his attention to the printing and publication of the book, and in the spring of 1830 the first edition of the Book of Mormon was given to the world.

5. IMPORTANT REVELATIONS.

To the Prophet Joseph, intelligence concerning the new Church which God was about to establish, was made known as it was needed, as the work progressed. The whole plan was neither revealed at once nor understood by the Prophet from the beginning. During his whole life he received numerous revelations through which he was taught, and by which he was prepared for his labors as they appeared. These counsels and teachings are found in the Doctrine and Covenants, a book of revelations given as necessity demanded for the comfort and guidance of the servants of God and the Church.

On one occasion, while engaged in the translation of the Book of Mormon, Joseph and Oliver encountered a passage which spoke of baptism for the remission of sins. This being new to them, as it is to many to this day, they felt a desire, a necessity to comply with this doctrine. After consulting on the matter, they went to the woods and there united in prayer for light on the subject. While thus engaged a heavenly messenger descended before them. He told them that he was John the Baptist, and that he had come to minister to them under the direction of the Apostles Peter, James and John, who still held the Priesthood after the order of Melchisedek. Laying his hands upon their heads, he conferred upon them the Aaronic Priesthood, which holds the keys of the ministering of angels, and the gospel of repentance and baptism by immersion for the remission of sins. The angel also instructed them in the duties of this Priesthood, saying that in due time the Higher, or Melchisedek Priesthood, without which there can be no true Church of Christ, would be conferred upon them by proper authority. John then commanded them to go forth and baptize each the other by virtue of the authority transmitted to them; this was accordingly done on the 15th day of May, 1829, when Joseph baptized Oliver and afterward Oliver immersed Joseph for the remission of sins. Coming out of the water, they ordained each other to the Aaronic Priesthood, following which the Holy Ghost fell upon them, causing them to rejoice and prophesy. Thus was the beginning made to the membership of the Church of Christ, the initiatory ordinance being performed by direct authority from heaven.

Time after time Joseph proclaimed to anxious enquirers the tidings that an angel from heaven had restored to earth the power to baptize men for the remission of sins, and that himself and Oliver had been the recipients thereof. Out of the scriptures he reasoned with his friends, as he met them. People soon began to receive the testimony, among the first being Samuel H. and Hyrum Smith, brothers of the Prophet.

After the removal to Fayette, several honest souls in the Whitmer family became convinced of the divine mission of the Prophet, and were baptized; while many others thereabout were soon made believers through the inspiration of the Spirit and by means of the instructions and persuasions of Joseph and Oliver, who were privileged to meet the people and speak to them on many occasions.

In the course of the work of translating the Book of Mormon, the Prophet and his scribe learned that the Lord would provide three special witnesses, who should be granted permission to see the plates, etc., and who should bear record of the same.* By revelation, Oliver Cowdery, David Whitmer and Martin Harris were chosen such witnesses.† Some days after their selection, these men with the Prophet retired into the woods to obtain a fulfillment of the promised privilege. In answer to their prayers, an angel appeared showing them the plates, turning over the leaves, one by one, so that they could see them and discover upon them the engravings. A voice said unto them that the plates had been revealed and correctly translated by the power of God. They were then commanded to bear record of what they saw and heard, which they afterward did, their testimony being found in every edition of the Book of Mormon. It remains unimpeached to this day, notwithstanding all of them subsequently apostatized, not one of them ever denied that he had seen the plates and the heavenly messenger as he had at first solemnly testified. Eight other witnesses, whose testimony is also found in all editions of the book, testify that Joseph showed them the plates which they handled.

At a day not definitely known, but between the 15th

---

*See Book of Mormon, Ether v, 2-4.
†See Section 17, Doctrine and Covenants.

of May and the end of June, 1829, Peter, James and John appeared in glory to Joseph, conferring upon him and Oliver Cowdery the Apostleship and Melchisedec Priesthood which these ancient disciples of the Lord and Savior held while in mortality. These two modern servants of God, the first Elder and the second in the Church, then re-ordained each other to the same Priesthood. The gift of the Holy Ghost was now sealed upon their heads, and they rejoiced exceedingly being now in position to confer this gift upon others. They were also thus made possessors of the Melchisedek Priesthood, which is the "moving, directing, controlling, governing or presiding agency, right and authority which is vested in the Godhead and delegated unto man for the purposes of his instruction, initiation into the Church, spiritual and temporal guidance, government and exaltation. * * * Which is without father, without mother or descent, or beginning of days or end of life; which the Great High Priest, Melchisedek, so honored and magnified in his time that it was called after his name, in honor to him and to avoid the too frequent repetition of the name of the Son of God."*

Following their ordination to the High Priesthood, came a momentous revelation from the Lord making known to them the calling of Twelve Apostles in the last days, giving also many instructions concerning the building up of the Church of Christ according to the fullness of the gospel.†

Thus, during the eventful months of May and June, 1829, were revealed many important truths and princi-

---

* Joseph F. Smith, in *The Contributor*, Vol. X, page 307.
† See Doctrine and Covenants, Section 18.

ples, fraught with world-wide benefits, with great consequences to the religious world.

It was learned that baptism is essential, and is for the remission of sins; and men were authorized to perform this ordinance.

Witnesses were chosen to testify to the divinity of the Book of Mormon, now almost ready to be distributed to the inhabitants of the world, who would through it receive a fullness and an undefiled explanation of the gospel of Jesus Christ as taught anciently.

The beginning was successfully made in proclaiming these tidings to mankind.

As a result of the whole, the hour was rapidly approaching when the true Church could be organized, when the "marvelous work and a wonder" which the Lord was in the act of bringing forth could be thoroughly founded in the earth.

II. FROM THE ORGANIZATION TO THE FLIGHT FROM KIRTLAND.

1830—1838.

1. ORGANIZATION OF THE CHURCH.

By the will and commandments of God, the 6th day of April, 1830, was the date fixed for the organization of the Church, for which everything was now in readiness. On that day a meeting of the baptized members, about forty in number, was called, and assembled in the house of Peter Whitmer, Sen., in Fayette, Seneca County, New York. The Church of Jesus Christ of Latter-day Saints was organized, on the date named, with six members, which number was required by law. The original members were: Joseph Smith, Jun., Oliver Cowdery, Hyrum Smith, Peter Whitmer, Jun., Samuel H. Smith and David Whitmer.

In conformity with previously revealed commandments, the Prophet Joseph, having first opened the meeting by prayer, called upon the members present to know whether they were willing to accept him and Oliver Cowdery as their teachers in the Kingdom of God, and whether they were willing to be organized as a Church. By unanimous vote they consented, whereupon Joseph laid his hands upon Oliver ordaining him an Elder in the Church of Christ, after which Joseph was ordained by Oliver to the same office. The sacrament of the Lord's Supper was partaken of by those who had been baptized, following which they were made the recipients of the Holy Ghost and confirmed members of the Church by the laying on of the Elders' hands. The Spirit was richly manifest, so that all rejoiced and praised God, while a number prophesied. Some of the brethren, for the members were now "brethren and sisters," were likewise, at this time, ordained to the various offices in the Priesthood, the duties of which were made known by revelation about this time.*

While the Saints were yet together on this occasion, the Prophet Joseph voiced to his followers the revelation found in the twenty-first section of the Doctrine and Covenants, in which his divine calling is declared, the forgiveness of his sins proclaimed, and the Church commanded to give heed, in all patience and faith, to his words as he shall receive them, as if they came from the mouth of the Lord Himself; being promised that in so doing, the Lord would disperse darkness from before them, cause the heavens to shake for their good, and that the gates of hell should not prevail against them. Mighty blessings are promised to those who shall labor in the vineyard to declare the way open for the remission of sins, and Jesus crucified for the sins of the world.

"Thus was founded," says the Historian Whitney, "the Church of Jesus Christ of Latter-day Saints. Thus arose, as a system, what the world terms Mormonism, —universally regarded as the most remarkable religious movement of modern times; detested and denounced

---

*In the 20 h Section of the Doctrine and Covenants are found instructions concerning Church organization, government and discipline, the proper mode of baptism, the administration of the Sacrament, duties of officers and members, etc

throughout Christendom as a dangerous and soul-destroying imposture, but revered and defended by its disciples as the wonderful work of the Almighty, the veritable 'marvelous work and wonder' foretold by Isaiah and other ancient seers, which was to prepare the world, by the preaching of the restored gospel and the founding of the Latter-day Zion for Messiah's second coming and the advent of the Millennium."

2. MANIFESTATIONS AND PERSECUTIONS.

The Church was organized on a Tuesday, and the first public meeting thereafter was held at the house of Peter Whitmer, in Fayette, on the following Sunday, April 11th, 1830. Since the appointment for this gathering had gone forth in all the surrounding neighborhood, it was attended by a large number of people. On this occasion, Oliver Cowdery, under Joseph's direction, preached the first public discourse delivered by an authorized servant of God in the latter-day dispensation. Saints and strangers were greatly comforted, many of the latter seeking baptism and membership among the people of God. Six were added that day, followed by seven others on Sunday the 18th, all being baptized by Oliver Cowdery, in Seneca Lake.

During the latter part of the month of April Joseph visited the home of Mr. Joseph Knight, at Colesville, Broome County, New York, the gentleman who had so kindly aided him in the hour of need while engaged in translating the Book of Mormon. Mr. Knight and family, who were Universalists, received him kindly, reasoning calmly with him upon his religious views.

The Prophet held several meetings which created friends, enemies and numerous enquirers after the truth. Among those who attended regularly was Newel Knight, a son of Joseph Knight, who became so interested in the words of the Prophet that he promised to pray in meeting before his friends. When the time came, however, he could not be prevailed upon to do that, but instead retired into the woods, from which place he returned in an alarming condition of mind and body. Visiting him, Joseph found his visage and limbs distorted and twisted; and while the Prophet was yet there, his friend was caught up from the floor and tossed helplessly about the room. Through the power of the Spirit, Joseph saw that he was in the hands of the evil one, and that the power of God alone could save him from such tortures. Joseph succeeded in getting hold of his hand, when Newel requested that the devil which possessed him be cast out. Joseph replied: "If you know that I can, it shall be done," and then, almost unconsciously, the servant of God rebuked the destroyer, commanding him in the name of Jesus Christ to depart. Instantly, Newel cried out with joy, saying that he could see the devil leave the room and vanish from sight. His countenance became natural, his distortions ceased, he was filled with the Holy Ghost, he believed, was made whole, and was afterward baptized by David Whitmer, while on a visit to Fayette in the latter part of May. Many others who witnessed this strange event subsequently became members of the Church.

Thus was the first miracle performed in the Church, by the power of God, and it was a beginning of the realization of the promises made,—for it was to be a gospel of "signs" following the believer, as in days of old. Since then, thousands of miracles have been, and are being performed by the Elders who ever give to the Father the praise, honor and glory.

Having completed his labors in Colesville, Joseph returned to Fayette, where he found much excitement over the coming forth of the Book of Mormon, which, though having been in print for some time, "was accounted a strange thing." The Saints, their friends, and believers in the book, were being subjected to much petty persecution.

In Fayette, on the first day of June, 1830, the first conference of the Church was held. Thirty members were present on the opening day, there being also many strangers, and believers in the new faith. The Sacrament was administered; the faith of the congregation was so great that many saw heavenly visions, and felt the manifestations of the Spirit in such a miraculous manner that they were deprived of their natural strength for a time. Restored to their bodily powers, they shouted "Hosannas to God and the Lamb," and rehearsed the glories which they beheld while yet in the Spirit. Many baptisms followed, more were ordained to the offices of the Priesthood, the brethren were inspired with fresh zeal in the cause, and Mormonism began spreading with unprecedented rapidity.

Returning immediately after this conference to his home in Pennsylvania, Joseph soon thereafter departed thence, with his wife, on a visit to the home of Joseph Knight, at Colesville, where he found many believers anxious for baptism. On a Saturday night, the Elders constructed a dam over a stream, where baptisms were to be performed after the appointed meeting on the following Sabbath day. But a mob, led by certain priests in the neighborhood, tore away the dam, necessitating the postponement of the ordinance till Monday, when, notwithstanding the rage of their eneimes, (who had become still more embittered at hearing the testimonies of the divinity of the Book of Mormon, and the first principles of the gospel, at the Sunday meeting,) thirteen persons were baptized under the hands of Oliver Cowdery. Among these was Emma, the wife of the Prophet Joseph, whose joy at welcoming her into the fold was unspeakable.

Scarcely was the ordinance completed, when the mob again began their annoyances. Fifty men surrounded the house of Mr. Knight, and it was only by exercising great care that the Elders were saved from violence. Joseph confronted the mob, bravely answering their insults and threatenings, in a vain endeavor to pacify them. Finally the rabble withdrew, and the Elders prudently went to the home of Newel Whitney. Here, as they were about to confirm the gathered converts, a constable appeared with a warrant for the arrest of Joseph, the charge being preaching the Book of Mormon and setting the country in an uproar. The arrest had been instigated by the mob whose plan was to get him into their hands, so the now friendly constable said. This proved to be true, and but for the friendliness of the officer, who found Joseph a different personage from what he had been represented, undoubtedly they would have taken him from custody. When the mob surrounded the wagon, the constable whipped up his horse, and thus drove the Prophet out of their reach. Taking him to South Bainbridge, Chenango County, he was lodged in a tavern where the constable kept watch over him for the night. Next day, amid great excitement, he was called for trial, the charges, among others, being that he had obtained from Josiah Stoal, his former employer, a horse, and from a Jonathan Thompson, a yoke of oxen, by telling them that he had received revelations that he was to have the property. Taking the witness stand, these gentlemen testified in the prisoner's favor, and he was promptly acquitted. His defenders were Messrs. Joseph Davidson and John Reid who had been secured by Mr. Joseph Knight.

No sooner was Joseph set free than he was re-arrested on a warrant from Broome County, and taken to Colesville for trial. The officer into whose hands he now fell treated him harshly, allowing him neither food nor water for many hours. At the tavern, the rabble abused, ridiculed, insulted, spit upon and pointed their fingers at him. Then at length he was given some crusts of bread and water, and permitted to retire for the night.

At the trial the following day, the same gentlemen defended him as were at the former trial. They held forth in its true light the malicious nature of the prosecutors of the case. Joseph was again promptly acquitted, there being no cause for action. This greatly angered his enemies who now threatened him with violence.

They were prevented from accomplishing their designs by the officer who had before treated him so harshly, but who, like many others who had witnessed the case, was now disposed to be friendly. With this help Joseph and his wife escaped unharmed to his home in Pennsylvania.

Not many days after, however, he, with Oliver Cowdery, revisited Colesville to confirm the baptized members, but scarcely had they arrived at the residence of Mr. Knight when the mob began to gather, and they were forced to flee for their lives, without accomplishing their purpose. On a subsequent visit they were more successful.

With the assistance of his wife and John Whitmer, Joseph now spent some time in arranging and copying the relvelations received up to this date. In the month of June, what is konwn as the "Visions of Moses,"* and in July the commandments found in the 24th, 25th and 26th sections of the Doctrine and Covenants were made known.

Oliver Cowdery had returned to Mr. Whitmer's, at Fayette, and while Joseph was yet in Harmony he received a letter from him, in which the announcement was made that an error had been discovered in one of the commandments, which Joseph was asked to correct, to which the Prophet replied that the words were given of God, and must stand as written until God should change them.†

It was only after Joseph had made a personal visit to Fayette that Oliver and some of the Whitmer family, who had also been misled, were convinced of the correctness of the Prophet's position; but even then the incident caused a breach between the First Elder and the Second, whose relations up to this time had been congenial and mutually helpful, which only temporarily closed, soon to be re-opened.

In the early part of August, some of the unconfirmed members, baptized in Colesville, came to Harmony, whereupon Joseph prepared to hold a confirmation meet-

---

*See "Pearl of Great Price," page 1.

† See Doctrine and Covenants, Section 20, verse 37, the words enclosed in commas in the last four lines.

ing. Wishing to administer the sacrament, he set out to obtain some wine, when he was met by a heavenly messenger, and received a revelation in which the use of wine in the sacrament is forbidden, unless it be made new among the Saints themselves.* Returning, Joseph complied with the instructions, the meeting being held as contemplated.

Persecutions now revived in Harmony, set in motion by the efforts of a Methodist minister. Joseph's father-in-law, Mr. Isaac Hale, was prevailed upon to join the ranks of the opponents, and from that time on became a bitter foe to Mormonism. It became impossible for Joseph and Emma to remain in their old home in Harmony, and so, accepting a second invitation from the Whitmers, they removed to Fayette, arriving there in the latter part of August, 1830.

3. MISSION TO THE LAMANITES.

Fresh troubles now confronted the cause. Upon arriving in Fayette, the Prophet found serious dissensions among his followers. The trouble arose over a stone in the possession of Hiram Page, through which he had obtained a number of spurious revelations, the teachings of which were contrary to the doctrines of the New Testament and to those received by the head of the Church. A number of the Saints had been misled, prominent among whom were Oliver Cowdery and some of the Whitmer family. Speaking in the name of the Lord, the Prophet told them that Satan had deceived Hiram

---

* Sect on 27, Doctrine and Covenants, verses 1-4.

Page, that the communications received through the stone were not of God, and that he alone was to receive revelations for the Church, until another should be appointed in his stead. All things were to be done in order, and by common consent by the prayer of faith. Oliver Cowdery was called upon to induce Page to discard the stone, and he was likewise called to preach the gospel to the Lamanites, which mission he was to fill as soon as the differences then existing in the Church were settled.* In this same revelation allusion is made to a "city" which, though not definitely located, was to be founded somewhere in the West, on the "borders by the Lamanites." It was about this time also that the important revelation concerning the eventual gathering of the Saints was given.†

At a three days' conference in Fayette, the second held in the Church beginning September 1st, 1830, Hiram Page and his associates renounced the stone in question, and all things connected therewith, renewing their fealty to Joseph as their leader and prophet. Thus harmony was restored once more, the threatened schism being completely blotted out. At this conference two revelations were given (Doctrine and Covenants, Sections 30 and 31) calling a number of the brethren on missions; and soon after its adjournment preparations were made for introducing the gospel to the Lamanites, or Indians, in conformity with the revealed word.

The Latter-day Saints believe that they themselves are of Israel, and it is a cardinal doctrine with them that scattered Israel shall be gathered in the last days,

---

* Doctrine and Covenants, Section 28.

† Doctrine and Covenants, Section   See also Section 10, vs. 59-65.

which in a measure accounts for the startling sacrifices made by them in proclaiming the gospel to all the nations of the earth, and in their calling upon the honest in heart, the seed of Israel, to gather to the land of Zion, or America. With Jeremiah they believe that "He that scattered Israel will gather him, and keep him, as a shepherd doth his flock." Hence their eagerness to declare the word of the Lord to the nations, and in the "isles afar off." The gathering, which involves not only the scattered remnants of Israel, but also the return of the Ten Tribes from the "north country," the restoration of the Jews, and the re-building of Jerusalem, was accounted a strange doctrine when first announced in this age; so was the calling of missionaries to go forth to preach without purse or scrip. Even the inspired mind of the Prophet scarcely understood, nay, did not understand, the full import of these and other doctrines revealed through his instrumentality. But he made this motto his rule of life: "When the Lord commands, do it," at the same time showing his followers the necessity of a like obedience.

The Indians, according to the belief of the Saints, which is founded upon the statements of the Book of Mormon, are a branch of the House of Israel, and are therefore to hear the word of God so that they may carry out their portion of the great gospel programe, and assist in buidling up the city of Zion, the New Jeursalem of the West. Hence the calling of missionaries at this early day to present the true gospel to them, together with the Book of Mormon, a record of the hand dealings of God with their forefathers.

The men selected by revelation* to perform this first distant mission, "to go into the wilderness, through the western states, and into the Indian territory," were Oliver Cowdery, Peter Whitmer, Jr., Parley P. Pratt and Ziba Peterson. While they were specially called to the Indians, they were nevertheless to preach wherever opportunity offered.

Parley P. Pratt, whose history at this point is inseparably interwoven with that of the Church, was born April 12th, 1807, in Burlington, Otsego County, New York, and was baptized into the Church by Oliver Cowdery, in Seneca Lake, September 1st, 1830. Previously he had been a Campbellite preacher. The Cambellites were a sect of reformed Baptists, whose stronghold was in and about Kirtland, Ohio, and the shores of Lake Erie. Among their noted men were Alexander Campbell, the founder of the sect, and Sidney Rigdon, a gifted expounder of the Scriptures. Soon after joining this sect, in August, 1830, Pratt decided to devote his life to the ministry, for which reason he sold his frontier home in Ohio, going east to carry out his resolve. While on this journey he first saw the Book of Mormon, in which he immediately became deeply interested. He started to seek the Prophet, but not finding him at home, he visited his brother Hyrum Smith, who accompanied him to Fayette, where, becoming convinced of the divinity of Joseph's mission, he was baptized as stated. He then went east and there converted his brother Orson, afterwards a famous Apostle and one of the pioneer founders of Utah. Returning west, he met the Prophet Joseph at Manchester, being soon

---

*Doctrine and Covenants, Section 28, 30 and 32

thereafter called to fill the before-mentioned mission to the Lamanites, or Indians.

Late in October, the four Elders began their westward journey on foot, trusting in the Lord "to open up the way." Near Buffalo, they presented their interesting message to the Catteraugus Indians, giving them copies of the Book of Mormon. They were kindly received by the red men. Continuing their journey, their next stop was at Kirtland, then a prosperous frontier town of about two thousand inhabitants, a city where "Mormonism itself, their parent Church, was destined soon to plant its pilgrim feet." Seeking an interview with his former teacher, Sidney Rigdon, Elder Pratt delivered to him the message of his new-found truths. Mr. Rigdon, with many of his prominent followers, among whom may be mentioned Edward Partridge and Newel K. Whitney, afterward the first two Bishops of the Mormon Church, soon became convinced that they had no authority to minister in the ordinances of God, hence were not legally baptized and ordained. Consequently many of them submitted to baptism at the hands of Elder Pratt and his associates, through whose ministrations they received the gift of the Holy Ghost by the laying on of hands. The interest and excitement over the new missionaries became general in the surrounding region. Night and day they were busy teaching the multitudes who came to listen. In two or three weeks after their arrival, one hundred and twenty-seven souls were baptized, which number soon increased to one thousand. The new converts "were filled with joy and gladness; while rage and lying were abundantly manifested by gainsayers; faith was strong, joy was great, and persecution heavy."

Ordaining Sidney Rigdon, Isaac Morley, John Murdock, Lyman Wight, Edward Partridge and many others, many of whom afterward became noted in the chronicles of the Church, to the ministry, to take charge of the Saints and minister the gospel, the successful missionaries, having first notified the Prophet of their progress, proceeded westward, adding to their number a new convert, Frederick G. Williams.

At Sandusky, in Western Ohio, the Wyandots were visited, which tribe rejoiced in the strange tidings revealed to them of their forefathers, and of the restored gospel. They were very friendly and bade the Elders God-speed to the West, in which direction the red men expected soon to follow.

Thence, the missionaries proceeded to Cincinnati and St. Louis where they met with little or no success. In passing his old forest home, some fifty miles from Kirtland, Elder Pratt was arrested on some trivial charge, but sagaciously made his escape. Near St. Louis they halted, owing to the dreadful storms, snow being three feet deep. With the opening of the new year, 1831, they continued their journey, traveling on foot three hundred miles through prairies covered with trackless wilds of snow, without shelter or fire, having for food frozen corn bread and raw pork. At length Independence, Jackson County, in the extreme western frontier of Missouri, was reached. So far the missionaries had been absent four months, they had traveled about fifteen hundred miles, through a comparative wilderness, mostly on foot, in the worst season of the year. They had preached the gospel to tens of thousands of their own race, and to two nations of Indians, besides having confirmed many hundreds and organized them into branches of the Church.

Two of the brethren remained at tailor work in Independence, while Elder Pratt and Cowdery crossed the frontier to the Indians, tarrying one night with the Shawnees; after which they crossed the Kansas River to the Delawares. Seeking the aged chief of this nation, a polygamist and sachem of ten tribes, the missionaries presented their message to him by means of a friendly interpreter. They were received kindly. After some hesitancy, on the part of the chief, a council was called, and Oliver Cowdery was permitted to address the Indians. Presenting them with a copy of the Book of Mormon, he gave an account of its history, and of the restoration of the gospel. For several days they remained to instruct the aborigines whose interest became intense, the excitement spreading to the whole tribe. Finally the ministers and agents on the frontier heard of the excitement, and through them the Elders were ordered out of the Indian country as peace-disturbers, threatened with military interference in case of non-compliance with the order. Under these circumstances, they reluctantly departed from among the Indians, returning to labor among the white settlers in Jackson County, where they met with some success.

At a council of the five Elders, held in Independence, on the 14th of February, 1831, it was decided to send Elder Pratt east to report their labors to the Prophet Joseph. Departing on this perilous journey, Elder Pratt, after much suffering, reached Kirtland, to which city the Prophet had now removed. Upon his arrival in March, 1831, the Lamanite missionary was there greeted with a hearty reception.

4. REMOVAL OF THE CHURCH TO OHIO.

Meantime, the cause of Mormonism had rapidly progressed in the east, through the ministrations of the Prophet and his associates. In the fall of 1830, Joseph had been visited by Orson Pratt, also by Sidney Rigdon and Edward Partridge of Kirtland, which latter reported the condition of that branch to the Prophet leader. These visitors came to enquire of the Prophet what was the will of the Lord concerning them.*

Sidney Rigdon was retained to assist Joseph as scribe in the inspired translation of the Holy Bible, which work was begun just before the close of the year 1830.

Already, as we have seen, it had been intimated that the West was the future field for Mormonism, and with the success of the Lamanite missionaries in Kirtland, it became evident to Joseph that the time was ripe for a general movement of the Church towards the land of their future destiny. The visit of Sidney Rigdon confirmed this idea. The site of the new "city" had not yet been definitely determined, but Kirtland would be a good resting place, where a flourishing Stake of Zion could be established, until such a time as God should reveal the location of the Zion which was to be "called the New Jerusalem, a land of peace, a city of refuge, a place of safety for the Saints of the Most High God." In Kirtland, in the meantime, the Saints might rest and gather strength.

Then came the first direct command for the Saints to gather,—the revelation which heralded the beginning of the gathering of Israel in the latter days. In it the

---

*Doctrine and Covenants, Sections 34, 35, and 36.

Church is commanded to "assemble together on the Ohio."* But before going, Joseph and Sidney were first to preach and strengthen the Saints in.the region round about, and more especially in Colesville, where the Saints were very faithful. This was done.

Preparatory to the emigration westward in compliance with the will of the Lord, a farewell gathering, the third conference of the Church, was held at Fayette, January 2nd, 1831. On this occasion, all the affairs of the Church in the east were settled, or left with trusted agents to arrange as speedily as possible. During the conference, the Lord made known to the Saints through revelation that a land of promise should be given them, which they should inherit forever on certain conditions.† In Ohio, in the mean time, they were promised that the law of God should be given to them, and that they should be endowed with power from on high.

Then the movement began. Toward the latter part of the month, the Prophet with his wife, accompanied by Sidney Rigdon, Edward Partridge, and others, left on their journey to Kirtland, where they arrived about February 1st, 1831. Joseph introduced himself to Mr. Newel K. Whitney as "Joseph the Prophet," and was by this gentleman kindly received and entertained. For several weeks himself and wife resided at the home of Mr. Whitney, where Joseph's time was occupied with important matters that pertained to the setting of the Church in order.

Shortly after the Prophet's arrival in Kirtland, the Saints in New York began to migrate. They reached

---

* Doctrine and Covenants, Section 37.
† Doctrine and Covenants, Section 38

their destination in May and June following, and settled in the northern part of Ohio, principally in and about Kirtland. The Ohio Saints were commanded to receive their "eastern brethren,"* and divide their lands with them, until the Lord should further direct the location of their land of inheritance.

5. THE LAW OF CONSECRATION.

Following the departure of the Lamanite missionaries from Kirtland, strange notions and false spirits had crept into the Church in this branch, which Joseph now immediately sought to eradicate and drive out, in which work he soon succeeded by the exercise of wisdom and caution.

It appears that the Campbellites, evidently with a desire to be like the early Christians who had all things in common, had organized in what was called the "common stock" plan of living. All dwelt together as a family, and the "family" nearly all joined the Church. Joseph induced them to abandon this plan for the more "perfect law of the Lord," which was consecration, or the United Order, which now became a law to the whole Church.

The provisions of this law, in short, were these: On entering the Order each individual was to consecrate all his property to the Bishop, utterly relinquishing its possession. The Church would then give a deed conveying to such person certain property as a stewardship for himself and family, of which he was to render an account to the Bishop. Every man was to seek the interest of his neighbor, there was to be no idleness, all would be

---

* Doctrine and Covenants, Section 48.

owners alike, yet each steward was free in the management of his stewardship, temporal equality was to be inaugurated. The key-note of the order is thus given by the Prophet: "It is not given that one man should possess that which is above another." It was to be a system like that of the Apostles at Jerusalem: "The multitude of them that believed were of one heart and of one soul,—neither said any of them that aught of the things which he possessed was his own; but they had all things common." It was to be a system such as prevailed in the "City of Enoch:" the Lord called his people Zion, because they were of one heart and one mind and dwelt in righteousness, and there was no poor among them."*

The first movement towards the establishment of this law was the organization of the Bishopric, the presidency of the Aaronic Priesthood, which has authority to minister in temporal things. The first Bishop called by revelation† was Edward Partridge, who "was appointed by the voice of the Church and ordained a Bishop" on the 4th day of February, 1831. He was to relinquish his business as merchant, and spend all his time in the service of the Church.‡

---

* For interesting discussions on this topic, see Whitney's "History of Utah," Vol. 1, page 82-85; Roberts' "Outlines of Ecclesiastical History," pp. 353-356; also Sections 42 and 51, Doctrine and Covenants.

† Doctrine and Covenants, Section 41.

‡ For complete organization of the Bishopric and its duties, see Roberts' "Outlines of Ecclesiastical History," pp. 346-350. Also, Doctrine and Covenants, Section 42, verses 30-32; and Section 51, verses 3-6 and 13-17. These quotations contain also a general outline of the Order which was introduced and sought to be established among the Saints in Kirtland, Ohio, and subsequently in Missouri.

Some days after the appointment of a Bishop, a revelation, found in the 42nd Section of the Book of Covenants, was given in which the Saints are taught important doctrines concerning the order, and the government of the Church.

All the Elders, except the Prophet and Sidney Rigdon are afterward commanded to go out, two by two, to preach the gospel, warning their converts to flee to the West. The Lord promises to reveal the location of the New Jerusalem in His own due time, for which the Saints were instructed to pray.

Thus was the law of consecration, the Order of Enoch, or the United Order, given to the Saints; but owing to persecutions, and to the selfishness, pride and disobedience of men, it was not permanently founded. With the Saints it is one of the still unsettled problems of the future, since the Lord has said that without it, Zion cannot be built.* The Church failed to live up to the order of God in this law, and hence, the lesser law of tithing was given them in lieu thereof, in the year 1838. This law requires the person to pay first his surplus property to the Bishop, and after that one-tenth of his annual income.†

---

6. LOCATING THE LAND OF ZION.

On the 6th day of June, 1831, the fourth general confernce of the Church was held in Kirtland, the scattered Elders attending agreeable to the call by revelation.‡

---

* Doctrine and Covenants, Section 105, verse 5.
† Doctrine and Covenants, Section 119.
‡ Doctrine and Covenants, Section 44.

The number of the Saints had now swelled to about two thousand souls. Great power was manifested in this gathering. The first High Priests were ordained, and the power of the Melchisedec Priesthood was more fully manifested than had been the case heretofore. Only Joseph and Oliver up to this time had held a position in this Priesthood higher than a common Elder, which office is an appendage to the Melchisedec Priesthood.

Many of the Elders were commissioned to go forth, two by two, to preach and baptize, as did the Apostles anciently.* They were to go upon different routes, journeying towards the Missouri frontier, organizing branches wherever the people would listen to their gospel message. They were to meet in the State of Missouri where the next conference of the Church was to be held, and at which time, if faithful, the location of their land of inheritance would be made known to them.

Shortly after the conference, revelations were received for Sidney Gilbert,† and for Newel Knight, the latter being in relation to the Colesville branch of the Church, whose members were among the first to embrace the gospel, now temporarily located at Thompson, Ohio.

They were commanded to journey westward," unto the borders of the Lamanites."‡ They had broken the law which had been given to them in a previous revelation, and this was now declared "void and of none effect."§

Then followed revelations for W. W. Phelps, afterward a prominent member of the Church, and Thomas B.

---

* Doctrine and Covenants, Section 52.
† Doctrine and Covenants, Section 53.
‡ Doctrine and Covenants, Section 54.
§ Doctrine and Covenants, Section 51.

Marsh, afterward the president of the Twelve Apostles, who had come to learn from the Prophet the will of the Lord concerning them.*

Conforming to the commandment received during conference, Joseph, in company with Sidney Rigdon, Martin Harris, Edward Partridge, W. W. Phelps, Joseph Coe, and A. S. Gilbert and wife, started from Kirtland on the 19th of June on his first visit to the land of Missouri. They were followed by the Colesville branch, who this time obeyed the revelation. Other Elders who were called departed by different routes, bound for the same destination. Joseph's company, journeying by wagon, stage, canal-boat, steamer, and on foot, reached Independence, Missouri, about the middle of July. The meeting with Oliver Cowdery and his missionary associates was the occasion of great rejoicing, and according to the Prophet was "moistened with many tears."

Immediately after the arrival of Joseph, the location for the City of Zion, the central gathering place of the Saints, was first definitely made known.† Independence was the chosen site, and the spot for the temple was designated as lying westward, on a lot not far from the courthouse. According to the revelation, lands were to be purchased by the Saints, and the soil in the region was to be dedicated for the gathering of Israel, and for the building of the New Jerusalem. Sidney Gilbert was appointed a merchant, and an agent for land purchases, while Edward Partridge, assisted by two counselors, was chosen to "divide the Saints their inheritance," to be a

---

* Doctrine and Covenants, Section 55 and 56.
† Doctrine and Covenants, Section 57.

judge in Israel, to receive the consecration of properties, to assign stewardships, and to receive the Saints then on the way from Ohio.

On the 1st of August Sidney Rigdon was called by revelation to consecrate and dedicate to the Lord the land of Zion, to write a description thereof, and to prepare "an epistle and subscription" to obtain money for purchasing lands for an inheritance.

The first step toward founding Zion was taken on the 2nd day of August, 1831. On that day Joseph, assisted by eleven other men, the whole representing the Twelve Tribes of Israel, helped to lay a log for a house in Kaw Township, twelve miles west of Independence, in which locality the newly arrived Saints from Colesville were settling. Elder Rigdon then dedicated the land. The following day, the 3rd, witnessed the consecration of the temple site, after which, on the 4th, the fifth conference of the Church (the first in Zion) was held at the house of Joshua Lewis, in Kaw Township, most of the Saints being present. Revelations were given concerning the Sabbath, and the return of certain Elders to Kirtland, among whom were Joseph Smith, Oliver Cowdery, and Sidney Rigdon.*

Complying with the word of the Lord, the Prophet, in company with ten Elders, left for the East, on the 9th day of August. During the interesting and eventful journey two revelations were given which were full of counsel and instruction to the brethren.†

On the 27th they arrived safe and well in Kirtland.

Thus was Zion located and dedicated on the western

---

* Doctrine and Covenants, Sections 59 and 60.

† Doctrine and Covenants, Sections 61 and 62.

border line of civilization, a colony planted therein, a temple site selected, and a migratory stream of Saints set in motion in the direction of the "promised land." In this practically untrodden West, the Saints hoped to establish themselves in the City of their God, but they were destined to disappointment and much tribulation.*

7. PROGRESS IN KIRTLAND AND THE EAST.

The Prophet, assisted by Sidney Rigdon, soon after turned his attention to the translation of the Scriptures, which work had been stopped since the previous December. For this purpose he retired, with his wife and two infants, twins, which they had adopted in place of twins of their own that had died, to the quiet little town of Hiram, in Portage County, on September 12, 1831. They made their residence with John Johnson, a member of the Church, the father of the future Apostles, Luke S. and Lyman E. Johnson, and father-in-law to Orson Hyde, later also an Apostle.

While pursuing his literary labors in this quiet retreat, Joseph received many important reveations for the guidance of the Church. "The Lord's Preface to the Book of Commandments," and the revelation called the "Appendix" were given in November. In the latter part of the same month Oliver Cowdery and John Whitmer departed for Jackson County, whither W. W. Phelps had preceded them for the purpose of preparing to print the book of Doctrine and Covenants, and other publications. Interesting doctrines were about this time revealed

---

* Foretold in Doctrine and Covenants, Section 58, verses 2-5.

explaining the Revelations of St. John,* and the meaning of verse 14, chapter vii, Paul's First Epistle to the Corinthians,† etc.; likewise instructions concerning the Bishopric of the Church.‡ On the fourth day of December a second Bishop, Newel K. Whitney, was chosen for the Kirtland Stake of Zion.

Teachings were enunciated upon which are based a number of the religious doctrines of the Latter-day Saints. In the "Vision"‖ is set forth the doctrine of universal salvation, in different degrees of glory for all men save the "sons of perdition," upon the condition of justice and mercy, according to their faithfulness and obedience to the gospel of Christ, each person being judged according to his works, and receiving according to his knowledge and merits. Little children are saved by the blood of Christ. For the heathen who died without law there is hope; and even for the wicked, who are "thrust down to hell," there is escape, after they have paid "the uttermost farthing" in God's eternal punishment, which does not necessarily mean never-ending punishment, but punishment inflicted by the Eternal One. There were spirits kept in the prison house beyond, whom the Son visited, preaching to them the gospel. They would have the privilege of receiving the testimony of Jesus, and, accepting it, be judged according to men in the flesh.

Besides continuing his literary labors, the Prophet took active part in the ministry, attending a number of conferences, and instructing the Church verbally and by

---

* Doctrine and Covenants, Section 77.
† Doctrine and Covenants, Section 74.
‡ Doctrine and Covenants, Sections 68 and 72.
‖ Doctrine and Covenants, Section 76.

written epistles. The while, persecution did not abate. Ezra Booth, who had apostatized, was at this time writing his series of nine letters in the *Ohio Star*, against Joseph and the Mormons. They were the means of creating great prejudice against the Prophet and his cause, and not that alone, but persecution also. He and Sidney Rigdon were brutally treated by a mob, at Hiram, on the night of March 25th, 1832. Joseph was stripped, covered with tar, beaten, and an attempt was also made to force a bottle of *aqua fortis* down his throat. The next day, though scarred and wounded, found him preaching to a large congregation, many of whom had assisted in mistreating him the previous night. That day he baptized three new converts. Sidney Rigdon was delirious for some time after the outrage. But the mobocratic feeling became so rampant that the Prophet considered it wisdom to leave.

He then departed on his second visit to Missouri, in April, being joined on the way by Sidney Rigdon and Bishop Whitney. They took a circuitous rout to avoid the mob. Before Emma left Hiram, one of the twins died as a result of exposure on the night of the outrage upon her husband. This little one may be called the first martyr in the Church.

On his arrival in Independence, Missouri, April 24th, the Prophet was well received by the Saints but was pained to learn that their enemies were already beginning to heap upon the insults and annoyancs that were to end in their cruel exile from Jackson County.

Having visited and instructed among the Saints received an important revelation,* ordered three

---

* Doctrine and Covenants, Section 83.

thousand copies of the Doctrine and Covenants printed, and been acknowledged as president of the High Priesthood—to which office he had been ordained at the seventh general conference of the Church, in Amherst, Ohio, on January 25th—Joseph and his two companions started on their trip to Kirtland early in May. In Indiana, Bishop Whitney broke his leg, which delayed them one month in Greenville. At this place an attemp- was made to poison the Prophet, and he narrowly escaped death.

Arriving in Kirtland sometime in June, Joseph spent the season working upon the translation of the scriptures. His son Joseph, now leader of the Josephite, or re-organized church, was born on the 3rd of November of that year. In December the "revelation and prophecy on war"* was recorded which the Latter-day Saints claim was literally fulfilled in the great conflict between the Northern and the Southen States of the Union—the civil war.

Mormonism continued to prosper, branches being founded in various parts of the United States and Canada. During the winter of 1832-3, the school of the prophets was established, and a temple at Kirtland was projected, the corner-stones of which were laid on the 23rd of July following. The translation of the New Testament was completed on the 2nd of February, 1833, and the manuscript sealed to be opened in Zion.

Many revelations of great consequence to the Church were made known.†

On the 18th day of March, 1833, the first Presi-

---

* Doctrine and Covenants, Section 87.
† See Doctrine and Covenants, Section 88 to 92.

dency, the highest presiding quorum in the Church, was first organized, with the following *personnel:* Joseph Smith, President; Sidney Rigdon, first Counselor; Frederick G. Williams, Second Counselor.

Prosperity smiled upon the cause in Kirtland and the east. Over $11,000.00 worth of land was purchased upon which the Saints were to build and beautify the city, now surnamed "Shinehah," while awaiting further developments in Missouri, "the land of Zion." Workshops, mills and public buildings, were erected, and various industries established.

8. EXPULSION FROM JACKSON COUNTY.

In the midst of this prosperity, Oliver Cowdery arrived in Kirtland in the beginning of September, 1833, a messenger from the Saints in Missouri, bringing the sad news of the serious disturbances and persecutions in Jackson County.

There were now about twelve hundred Saints in Missouri, which number was being augmented constantly by immigration. They had improved their purchased lands, established industries, reaped rich harvests; they had a paper called the *Evening and Morning Star*, edited by W. W. Phelps, established in June, 1832; Parley P. Pratt presided over a school of sixty Elders, and the gospel was being preached to the people thereabouts with success. The Saints were thrifty, industrious, tended their own affairs, in short, "minded their own business," a standard creed with the Mormons. They doubtless had faults, and some were indiscreet. Blinded by their own ideas, perhaps others said things that were not wise, gave utterance to sentiments which offended the people not of their faith, but where such was the case, it was in violation of the teachings of their religion which inculcated the principles of living at peace with all men. They were law-abiding and peaceable citizens.

There being no law that would rid them of the Mormons, it was wickedly determined that this should be done without law. As early as April of this year, a meeting was called to devise means as to the best way to dispose of the Mormons. That gathering was unsuccessful, but another, held about the middle of July succeeded. At this meeting in Independence, some three hundred persons met to devise a plan for expelling the Saints. They signed a declaration accusing the Mormons of blasphemy, pretensions to miracles and healing the sick, casting out devils, and tampering with the negro slaves and the Indians, and declaring the Indian country to be theirs by heavenly inheritance. Later, at a meeting of five-hundred of the mob, on the 20th, the above charges were reiterated, others being added, and it was resolved that the Mormons leave the country forthwith, that no Mormon be allowed to settle there in the future, and that the printing of the *Star* be suspended. A committee was appointed to inform the Mormon leaders of this decision. The latter asked for time to consider. This only aroused the fury of the mob, who immediately gathered around the printing office, tore it down and scattered the material through the street. Other outrages followed. Bishop Partridge was covered with tar and feathers, and others of the Saints were threatened and abused. Clergymen and other prominent citizens took part in these lawless acts. Lieutenant-Governor L. W. Boggs said to some of the

Mormons: "You now know what our Jackson County boys can do, and you must leave the county."

Three days after these outrages were committed another larger meeting was held, another committee chosen. Realizing that their liberties were lost, that it was useless to withstand the rioters, the Saints entered into a peace agreement with the mob. They would leave the county—one half of them on January 1st, 1834, and the remainder on April 1st. The *Star* would be suspended; immigration would cease. In return for these concessions, the mob committee agreed, and the action was ratified by the meeting, that the Saints should be molested no more.

This was the message that Oliver Cowdery carried to Kirtland. In reply, the Prophet sent an epistle and messengers to comfort and advise the people in their unfortunate circumtances, but when they arrived in Missouri, in the latter part of September, they found that the mob had broken its pledge, and fresh outrages against the Saints were in progress.

"The Mormons must go," was the general cry. The Saints appealed to the State executive for military aid in vain. That functionary advised them to try the law. Following his advice brought only disaster. It was like applying fire to powder. Soon the whole country rose in arms to make war upon the unfortunate, peculiar people. It was on the 30th and 31st of October, and the 1st of November that the most furious attacks were made. Men were beaten, houses unroofed, property destroyed, women and children driven screaming into the wilderness.

Four of the Saints went to a circuit judge for a peace warrant, but were told that it would not be issued for fear of the mob. The judge advised them to "shoot down" the outlaws if these came again upon them. At the next onslaught the Saints prepared to carry out this advice, notwithstanding their repugnance to the taking of human life. On the 4th of November a battle ensued. One Mormon was killed, several were wounded, and two mobbers bit the dust. A general Mormon "uprising" was now heralded abroad. On November 5th, Lieutenant-Governor Boggs ordered out the militia to suppress the alleged insurrection. This only made matters worse. The mob was permitted to obtain what had been denied to the Saints—the militia. Boggs permitted the mob to enroll themselves among the troops. He demanded that the Mormons lay down their arms, and he seized a number of them to be tried for murder, telling the remainder to leave the country. To do this they had no time. Col. Pitcher, afterward court-martialed for his cruelty, turned his mob-militia upon the disarmed and helpless Saints; then followed scenes beggaring description. "Armed bands of ruffians ranged the county in every direction, bursting into houses, terrifying women and children and threatening the defenseless people with death if they did not instantly flee.   *   *   *   Out upon the bleak prairies, along the Missouri's banks, chilled by November's winds and drenched by pouring rains, hungry and shelterless, weeping and heart-broken, wandered forth the exiles. Families scattered and divided, husbands seeking wives, wives husbands, parents searching for their children, not knowing if they were yet alive."*

Thus were between twelve and fifteen hundred souls

Whitney's "History of Utah," Vol. I., p. 108.

expelled from their homes and possessions in Jackson County, three hundred of their houses burned, ten settlements left desolate. Most of the exiles found refuge in Clay County, just across the river, where they were kindly received.

The highest authorities in the state and nation were asked for redress, but the nation's executive could not interfere without petition from the state authorities, and the state authorities would do nothing because they were either in fear of or in sympathy with the mob. Leading, fair-minded citizens regarded the outrage as a grave stain upon the name of Missouri; but all in vain; to this day, without recompense, the Saints are dispossessed of their rightful inheritance in their promised Zion.

---

9. HIGH COUNCIL ORGANIZED.

In the latter part of November, messengers arrived in Kirtland giving details of the outrages that had been committed in Missouri. At this time all was not peace in Kirtland. The Prophet had been harrassed with lawsuits, and fears were even entertained for his life, so much so that trusty friends guarded him night and day. There were various other annoyances, among which may be mentioned the strife which Dr. Hurlburt, with his lying stories, succeeded in arousing by lecturing in various places round about. This Dr. Hurlburt had been excommunicated from the Church for immoral conduct; he it was who originated the theory of connecting the Book of Mormon with the Spaulding story, a theory now recognized as false by the best authorities outside of the

Church. and of course always declared to be false by the members of the Church.*

It was now decided to establish the printing press in Kirtland. Oliver Cowdery became editor of the *Star*.

On the 17th of February, 1834, an important step was taken. On that day the first High Council of the Church was organized.† It was composed of twelve High Priests, over whom three others of the same order were to preside. There is now a High Council in each of the thirty-three Stakes of Zion, each of which is presided over by the Presidency of the Stake‡—three High Priests who are themselves amenable to the First Presidency of the Church.

The duty of this council is to adjust difficulties between members of the Church, which have been brought up on appeal from the ward bishop's court. Cases are brought before the ward bishop's court by the "district" Teachers. The High Council has also original jurisdiction. The Council was appointed by revelation, and the object of its organization is to prevent strife and dis-

---

* President James H. Fairchild, in the "New York Observer" of February 5th, 1885, speaking of the discovery by Mr. Rice of the Spaulding Romance, says: "The theory of the origin of the Book of the Mormon in the traditional manuscript of Solomon Spaulding will probably have to be relinquished * * * Mr. Rice, myself and others compared it (the Spaulding manuscript) with the Book of Mormon, and could detect no resemblance between the two, in general or detail. There seems to be no name or incident common to the two. * * * Some other explanation of the origin of the Book of Mormon must be found, if any explanation is required."

† For the names of the High Priests composing this Council, and the duties of High Councils in general, see Doctrine and Covenants, Section 102.

‡ A "Stake" is a division of the Church presided over by a Council of three High Priests; a "Ward" is a division of a Stake, in which a Bishop and his two Counselors exercise supervision; a "District" is a division of a Ward in which presiding Teachers look after the interests of Church members

union, to assist the members of the Church to adjust their difficulties without costly litigation which the Mormon leaders do not favor among their followers. Excommunication from the Church is the extreme penalty decreed by this Council, while suspension from membership, or from the privileges of Church communion, and in certain cases excommunication, is the greatest punishment inflicted by the Bishop's court.

The order of adjusting difficulties, then, in the Church between members is this: If a person offend another, the person so offended shall go alone to the one who gave offense and tell him of his fault; if the offender confess, the offended shall be reconciled, if not, then witnesses shall be taken, and if still there is no reconciliation then the matter may be taken to the Bishop's court for settlement. From this court either party may make an appeal to the High Council, whose decision is final, and if not complied with, results in the guilty party losing his standing in the Church.*

---

10. ZION'S CAMP.

Early in the spring of 1834, Parley P. Pratt and Lyman Wight, messengers from the Saints in Missouri, came to Kirtland to counsel with the Prophet regarding the exiled people of Zion, and if possible adopt some measure for their relief and the restoration of their rights. The result of their visit was a further mission east for reasons set forth in the 101st and 103rd sections

---

* Doctrine and Covenants, Section 42, verses 8 to 91. Roberts' "Ecclesiastical History," pp. 386-389. Matt. xviii. 15-17.

of the Doctrine and Covenants; and finally, the assembling of about two hundred men, with twenty wagons laden with supplies, to carry provisions to the Saints in Missouri, to reinforce and strengthen them, and if possible to influence the Governor to restore to them their rights. They were also to "redeem Zion," or, in other words, seek to regain possession of the lands from which they had been driven in Jackson County. This company of men were organized as a military body, led by the Prophet in person, as general, and was known as Zion's Camp.

On the 5th of May, one hundred men departed from Kirtland for Missouri, and the remainder, to the number of two hundred and five, were recruited on the way. Composed of the young and middle-aged men — the strength of the branches of the Church in the east — there were many Elders in this expedition who afterwards became pillars of great strength in the Church. Among the most prominent of these may be named Brigham Young, Heber C. Kimball, Wilford Woodruff, Orson Pratt, Jedediah M. Grant and George A. Smith.

The news of their coming, supplemented with exaggerated reports of their strength and intentions, created considerable excitement in Missouri. Their enemies armed to attack them. One night on Fishing River, the Camp was saved from their foes by a severe storm which swelled the stream so that it became impassable. Military aid was sought from the Governor, who at first seems to have promised to call out the militia to reinstate the exiles, but afterward said that he had no authority to keep a force to protect them after they were restored, which in other words meant a refusal to do anything for them. Afterward prominent citizens visited the Camp, and learned that the Prophet's intentions were peaceable. He only wished to amicably adjust the difficulties between the county and his followers.

Among the members of the Camp at one time dissensions arose, and for their disobedience and rebellions the Prophet severely reprimanded some of them, predicting that a scourge would come upon the Camp because of their folly. On the 22nd of June, cholera broke out in their midst, in fulfillment of his prediction. Sixty-eight were attacked, thirteen died.

At Rush Creek, on the 25th of June, the Camp was disbanded. Negotiations were entered into between the Mormon leaders and the men of Jackson County. The latter offered to purchase the land from which the Saints had been driven, but the Mormons declined, deeming it sacrilege to dispose of their "sacred inheritance." Then the Saints made a counter proposal to purchase the land of those who did not wish to live neighbors to them in peace, promising that it would be paid for within a year. This offer their opponents rejected, intimating that it would be better for them to look for a new home in the wilderness beyond the distant County of Clinton.

For their possessions in Jackson County the Saints received nothing but threats and beatings. In Clay they found a peaceful home where they prospered for about three years, during which time affairs in Kirtland were shaping for rich spiritual blessings, as well as for the fearful financial crash and apostasy of 1837, which came near culminating in the destruction of the Church.

The Prophet and his associates returned to Kirtland on the 9th of July, 1834, after having organized, on the

3rd inst., a High Council in Clay County, with a Stake Presidency to take charge of Church affairs in Missouri.*

11. APOSTLES AND SEVENTIES CHOSEN.

If it be conceded that Zion's Camp failed in accomplishing the ostensible purposes for which it was organized, it cannot be denied that it was a success in trying the mettle of its members. A journey of over two thousand miles on foot, in rain and mud, exposed to sickness and death, is sufficient to prove the temperament, courage and fortitude of any person who may engage in it. Possibly this was one of the objects the Prophet had in view, as might be inferred from the next important measure which he was inspired to adopt—the choosing of the Twelve Apostles, the quorum next in authority to the First Presidency.

On the 14th of February, 1835, the survivors of Zion's Camp were called together, and from their numbers were chosen, by the Three Witnesses to the Book of Mormon, Twelve Apostles, each of whom was blessed and set apart by the First Presidency, the whole being in conformity with the word of the Lord received as early as June, 1829.†

The names of the quorum of Twelve were: Thomas B. Marsh, David W. Patten, Brigham Young, Heber C.

---

* The Stake Presidency were: David Whitmer, Wm. W. Phelps, and John Whitmer.

The members of the High Council: Simeon Carter, Parley P. Pratt, William E McLellin, Calvin Beebe, Levi Jackman, Solomon Hancock, Christian Whitmer, Newel Knight, Orson Pratt, Lyman Wight, Thomas B. Marsh and John Murdock.

† Doctrine and Covenants, Section 18.

Kimball, Orson Hyde, Wm. E. McLellin, Parley P. Pratt, Luke Johnson, William Smith, Orson Pratt, John F. Boynton, and Lyman Johnson. These were chosen as special witnesses to preach the gospel to the nations of the earth, and the duty of the quorum, besides, was, as it is now, to build up the Church, to regulate its affairs under the First Presidency, to ordain and set in order all the officers in the Church, and to call upon the Seventy to assist them to fill calls for preaching and administering the gospel. They form a quorum equal in authority and power to the First Presidency, and stand next to them in presiding.*

Soon after the organization of the Twelve, the First and Second quorums of Seventies were likewise chosen from the surviving members of Zion's Camp. "These quorums, as would be inferred from their being called Seventies' quorums, consist of seventy men. Seven presidents preside over each quorum, and the first seven presidents—the presidents of the first quorum—preside over all the quorums of Seventies in the Church."† Up to 1892, there had been one hundred and seven quorums of this class organized in the Church, and the organization of more will continue, if it be required, "even until there are one hundred and forty and four thousand thus set apart for the ministry."‡

Early in May, the Twelve started upon their first mission to the Eastern States. The duties devolving

---

* Doctrine and Covenants, Section 107, verses 23 to 40 and 58, in which section is also found information regarding the duties and powers of the various councils and quorums of the Priesthood that govern the temporal and spiritual affairs of the Church.

† Robert's "Outlines of Ecclesiastical History," p 368.

‡ So writes the Prophet Joseph, under date of May 2nd, 1835.

upon them were to preach, baptize, advise the scattered Saints to gather westward; and to collect means for the purchase of lands in Missouri, and for the completion of the Kirtland Temple.

About this time various secular and religious schools were established, which were widely attended by the leading Elders. In the winter of 1835-36, Mr. Joshua Seixas conducted a class in Greek, concerning the progress of which Joseph said that the Lord had opened their minds in a marvelous manner to understand His word in the original language. The Prophet had great taste for education, and, though unlearned at first, at the age of thirty he became quite proficient in language, philosophy and statesmanship. He was ever a staunch friend of progress and enlightenment which may with equal truth be said of his successors, and of the leaders of the Church in general, though the enemies of Mormonism aver the contrary, often asserting that the system fosters ignorance and is opposed to education. The educational precepts of the Prophet, which have become mottoes-in-practice with every Latter-day Saint, give the lie to their assertions: "It is impossible to be saved in ignorance;" "A man is saved no faster than he gets knowledge;" "The glory of God is intelligence;" "Seek ye out of the best books words of wisdom; seek learning even by study and also by faith."

It was about this time that the "Book of Abraham" was translated from papyrus found in the catacombs of Egypt. In August, 1835, the Prophet enunciated the views of himself and his people on civil government, found in full in the 134th section of the Doctrine and Covenants.

Immediately upon the return of the members of Zion's

Camp, the work on the temple in Kirtland, which had been hindered by their absence, was prosecuted with vigor and zeal, the Saints being anxious to receive the spiritual blessings which had been promised them upon the completion of the House of the Lord.* The Prophet supervised the work while leading Elders joined in pushing it to completion. It was finally dedicated on the 27th of March, 1836, though not entirely finished in the interior. Three years had been spent in its construction which had cost about $70,000.00. It was the first temple in modern times built by divine command. At that time the ordinance of baptism for the dead, with other vicarious work, one of the chief objects of temple-building with the Saints at present, had not been revealed. For that reason there was no baptismal font in the Kirtland temple. The main purpose of its erection was that other religious ordinances might be performed therein, and that there might be a House of the Lord in which spiritual blessings could be received, a place also for schools, meetings and councils of the Priesthood.

Upon the day of its dedication there was a time of general rejoicing, and thereafter many miraculous manifestations were witnessed therein,† some of which are named in the 110th section of the Doctrine and Covenants, and are in fulfillment of the words of the Prophet as recorded in the 4th chapter of Malachi. Some time after the dedication, according to the words of the

---

* Doctrine and Covenants, Section 105, verses 12 and 18; also Section 38, verse 32.

† See Jenson's "Historical Record," pp. 64 to 65, and 74 to 80.

Lord, the Twelve Apostles held the "Solemn Assembly," were endowed with power from on high, and received their "washings and anointings."

12. DEPARTURE FROM CLAY COUNTY.

After their expulsion from Jackson County, the Saints were received with some degree of kindness in Clay, where for about three years their industry and thrift caused the wilderness to blossom with abundance. Their numbers were greatly enlarged by immigrations from the east. It was considered, however, a temporary home, since they hoped to be re-instated in the lands from which they had been driven.

Until the summer of 1836 there had been no objection to them. They were peaceable, industrious, tended to their own affairs. But at that time the spirit of mobocracy re-appeared, wakened from its temporary slumber by the men of Jackson, who began crossing the river in squads to stir up strife and enmity. They even insulted and plundered their victims. The peaceable people of Clay, fearing a repetition of former difficulties, held a meeting in which they decided to advise the Saints to seek another home. This they did, having first reminded them under what circumstances they were received. There were objections to them, but these were mostly of a trivial character. Their dialect, manners and customs, were not like those of the Missourians, and it was even charged that they were non-slave holders or abolitionists. The state government was unfavorable to them. For his hostility to the Saints in their former trouble, Boggs had been made Governor of Missouri, and their most bitter enemies—Lucas and

Wilson—were given commissions as Major and Brigadier-Generals. It appeared now that the great majority of citizens in the state had joined with these officers in the determination that the Mormons should be prevented from enjoying any political, civil or religious rights, and they unitedly conspired to war against them as members of the commonwealth.

Viewing the situation aright, under these circumstances, the Saints now resolved for the sake of friendship, to be in a covenant of peace with the citizens of Clay County, and to show gratitude to those who had befriended them, to leave the county, notwithstanding this action involved an enormous sacrifice of property.

In September, 1836, they accordingly began moving to their new location in the Shoal Creek region, then a wilderness in Ray County, north-east of Clay. In December of the same year in answer to their petitions, this district was incorporated by the Legislature, and thus was Caldwell County created. To this place the Saints removed in large numbers, nearly all of them becoming land-holders, and it was there they founded the city of Far West, in the winter of 1836-7, which afterward became the county seat. Most of the officers of the city and county, elected according to the law, were Mormons. In this new home the exiles found a peaceful rest for a season, their numbers rapidly increasing until settlements were also made in Daviess County and elsewhere.

Following the wonderful spiritual manifestations enjoyed in the temple, there swept over Kirtland a wave of inflation, mistaken for temporal prosperity, which turned the heads of her inhabitants. A spirit of speculation permeated the whole community, playing havoc with the faith of the Saints and many of their leaders. All kinds of schemes were adopted to amass wealth, and the spirit of real estate speculations, so prevalent throughout the nation, took deep root in the Church. As a result there followed in quick succession evil-surmisings, fault-finding, disunion, dissensions, apostasy, and finally financial ruin. The Kirtland Safety Society Bank, established by Joseph for the benefit and advantage of the Saints, failed through the speculation, swindling and treachery of subordinate officers. The crash became general, and many of the people were utterly ruined financially.

Apostasy followed. The disaffected members became bitterly hostile to the Prophet, as if he were the cause of the very evils which he struggled most to avoid, and which were brought upon the people because they would not heed his counsels. About one-half of the Apostles, one of the First Presidency, and many leading Elders disloyally declared him to be a "fallen prophet," and themselves apostatized. The Church seemed threatened with utter destruction.

It was on the 1st of June, 1837, while these radical disturbances were in progress that the Lord revealed to Joseph that something must be done for the salvation of the Church. Up to this time there had been no missionaries sent to foreign lands. Proselyting had been confined to the eastern states, to Canada and a narrow district in the west. Now it was determined to open a mission in England. Apostle Heber C. Kimball was chosen to pioneer this work, his assistant and companion Apostle being Orson Hyde. Willard Richards was called later, and together they sailed from New York on the 1st day of July, 1837, to fill their mission. They were instructed to preach only the first principles of the gospel, which they did with much success. In less than a year they had organized twenty-six branches of the Church, with a membership of about two thousand souls. Throngs came to hear them, and whole villages were converted at a sweep. The opening of this mission was one of the most important events in the history of the Church—a grand movement destined to bring about 75,000 souls into its fold from England alone, and emigrate them to America. On their return, the Apostles landed in New York on the 12th of May, 1838. There they found a large branch of the Church which had been erected through the efforts of Parley P. Pratt and his brother Orson, the former having there published his celebrated work, the Voice of Warning, the year before.

But while the cause was thus prospering over the waters, in Kirtland flourished the destroying agencies of apostasy, persecution, confusion and mobocracy.

The Church in Missouri did not entirely escape the disaffection.. The local leaders lost the confidence of the people, necessitating a hurried visit of the Prophet to Far West, where he arrived November 1st, 1837. Having held a conference and arranged affairs in Missouri, he returned to Kirtland about December 10th. It was while absent that leading Elders in the latter place conspired to overthrow him, and to appoint David Whitmer in his stead. Among them were several of the Apostles and some of the witnesses of the Book of Mormon. Their schemes would have succeeded but for the fidelity and loyalty of Brigham Young, who defended the Prophet, exposed the evil designs of his enemies, and frustrated their plans.

John Taylor, also, later an Apostle and the third

President of the Church, who had come from Canada to Kirtland in the fall of 1837, stood loyal to the Church and to Joseph—as loyal as when seven years after he stood side by side with his Prophet-leader amid the bullet showers of Carthage jail, or as when fifty years later he died in cruel exile, a double martyr to the truth.

On the same grounds stood also the faithful veteran, Wilford Woodruff, who also became the beloved leader of the hosts of Israel.

At length, on December 22nd, Brigham Young, who persisted, publicly and privately, in declaring Joseph a true prophet of God, was forced to flee from Kirtland in consequence of the fury of the mobs. The new year opened with all the bitterness of the spirit of apostate mobocracy, which continued until the Prophet was compelled to seek safety in flight. He and Elder Rigdon left Kirtland on the night of January 12th, 1838, and were joined the next day by their families. They were followed more than two hundred miles by their armed pursuers, finally arriving in Far West on the 14th of March, 1838.

III. FROM THE MISSOURI EXODUS TO THE MARTYRDOM.

1838—1844.

1. BANISHED FROM MISSOURI.

The Prophet's flight was the signal for a general migration of the Saints from Ohio. The Kirtland Camp, composed of over five hundred souls soon thereafter made its way west.

The Saints in Missouri now numbered upwards of twelve thousand souls, most of whom were located in Caldwell, although there were thriving settlements in Daviess and Carroll Counties. Adam-ondi-Ahman,* where the Kirtland Saints rested and a stake of Zion was afterward organized, was the chief settlement in Daviess, and Dewitt in Carroll.

There were some divisions among the Saints when Joseph arrived, and vigorous measures were instituted to purge the Church of its disaffected members. At a Far West conference, a number of prominent men—among them Oliver Cowdery, David Whitmer, and the Johnsons—were excommunicated. Following this action, peace and prosperity again reigned. Several instructive revelations were received about this time, among which is one concerning the building of a temple at Far West, others about the duties of the Apostles and their mission

---

* See Doctrine and Covenants, Section 116; also Daniel VII, 9-14.

across the great waters, and the law of tithing.* For a few months, the Prophet spent his time in literary labors, enjoying peace with his people, instructing them, planning for their temporal and spiritual welfare.

About this time Joseph declared that the Lord had made known to him that Adam had dwelt in America, and that the Garden of Eden was located where Jackson County now is.

The lull of peace was only temporary, it was a calm before the storm. On the nation's birthday, 1838, a grand celebration was held at Far West, in which thousands of Saints participated. On that day the foundation stones of a temple were laid—a temple, however, destined not to be completed. Sidney Rigdon, the orator of the day, portrayed the suffering of the Saints, showing how their rights had been trampled upon; and, in a moment of enthusiasm, exclaimed: "We take God to witness, and the holy angels to witness this day, that we warn all men in the name of Jesus Christ to come on us no more forever. The man or the set of men who attempt it do it at the expense of their lives; and the mob that comes on us to disturb us, there shall be between us and them a war of extermination." His remarks were doubtless impolitic, but the provocation, and the enthusiasm of the day, should be considered as extenuating conditions.

The lightning which a day or two thereafter shivered their liberty pole, was as a precursor of the slumbering storm of human hate which was about to burst forth in pitiless fury over the unfortunate Saints. It was as an augury of the destruction of their own liberty.

---

* Doctrine and Covenants, Sections 113 to 120.

As in Jackson County, so here, the people feared the political rule of the Mormons.* The latter claimed their political rights—the right to vote for their friends. This was denied to them, and the result was a conflict which ended in their wholesale expulsion from the state of Missouri, in mid-winter, in the midst of outrage, robbery, massacre and suffering indescribable.

The trouble began at Gallatin, Daviess County, on the 6th of August, 1838. Twelve Mormons there tried to vote, the state election being then in progress. William P. Peniston, a candidate for the legislature, harangued a crowd against them. A tumult ensued. The Mormons cast their ballots, but several of them as well as a number of their opponents were wounded.

Reports of this trouble were exaggerated, and became a pretext for a general anti-Mormon uprising in the several counties. Threats were openly made and published, to drive the Mormons from the state. The conservative action of a number of leading citizens in signing a covenant of peace with the leaders of the Church, had no effect in calming the disturbance. The Missourians were in for war. Several hundred of the mob gathered in Daviess and Caldwell counties, some painted and disguised as Indians. Mormons were plundered, fired upon, and taken prisoners on false charges. There were housebreakings and other depredations until the situation became unbearable. Driven to this extremity, the Prophet now no longer counseled peace and submis-

---

* "Right or wrong, law or no law, and whether in accord with the letter or spirit of the constitution or government of the United States or not, the people of Missouri had determined that they would go any length before they would allow the Saints to obtain political ascendency in that quarter."—Bancroft's Utah, p. 117.

sion, but bade his followers protect themselves, their homes and little ones. The Saints armed to defend themselves, but were driven from Diahman, afterward from Dewitt, and from the outlying settlements in Caldwell, to Far West.

Col. Wight, a Mormon commissioned by General Parks of the state militia, organized a command, and, making vigorous war upon the marauders, succeeded in driving the enemy from Daviess County. This, of course only served to swell the excitement.

Then came the Crooked River battle, fought on the 25th of October. Captain David W. Patten led a force of Far West militia which attacked a band of marauders under Captain Bogart. The Mormons were victorious. Captain Patten and two of his men, however, were killed, while the enemy lost one man. The excitement, already at fever heat, now became intense. Governor Boggs who, when appealed to on a former occasion when the mob were victorious in plundering the Saints, had remarked that the quarrel was between the Mormons and the mob and that they might "fight it out," now that the Mormons were successfully defending themselves, changed his tactics, and saw his chance to wreak vengeance upon them. On October 27th, he issued an order to Major-General Clark, commanding the state forces, to proceed in all haste against the Mormons. They "must be treated as enemies, and must be exterminated or driven from the state if necessary, for the public good. * * * Instead, therefore, of proceeding as at first directed, to re-instate the citizens of Daviess in their homes, you will proceed immediately to operate against the Mormons." "Thus it appears that the Missouri state militia," says Bancroft, "called out in the first instance to assist the Mormon state militia in quelling a Missouri mob, finally joins the mob against the Mormon militia." And this, notwithstanding the Saints were in no wise opposed to the state, to law and to order. They were simply defending themselves by permission of the state.

At Richmond, two thousand troops under Major-General Samuel D. Lucas and Brigadier-General Moses Wilson were massed, and in the latter part of October departed for Far West. Elsewhere their commander, General Clark was mustering an army for the same purpose.

On October 30th, the frightful massacre of Mormons at Haun's Mill was perpetrated. A score of unoffending Mormons, men, women and children, lately arrived emigrants from the east, were cruelly killed and their bodies thrown into a well. This was done by a company of two hundred and forty men commanded by one Nehemiah Comstock.

On the same day Far West was beleaguered by the troops. Not having heard of the Governor's exterminating order, owing to the stoppage of their mails, the residents of the doomed city prepared to defend themselves, thinking the besiegers were a military mob.

It was at this critical juncture that Col. George M. Hinkle, commander of the Mormon forces, betrayed the Saints into the hands of their enemies by making an agreement with the besieging Generals in effect as follows:

The Mormons were to be disarmed, and their leaders were to be delivered up for trial and punishment. A deed of trust was to be executed pledging all Mormon property for the payment of the entire cost of the war.

The Mormons as a body, except the prisoners, were to forthwith leave the state.

These arrangements, made without the knowledge or consent of Hinkle's associates, or the leaders of the Church, were promptly, though cruelly on the part of the militia, carried into effect. Pretending to have arranged a conference between the Mormon leaders and the Generals, Col. Hinkle, on the 31st of October, without informing the former of his compact, delivered to General Lucas the following persons who were then treated as prisoners of war: Joseph Smith, Sidney Rigdon, Parley P. Pratt, Lyman Wight, George W. Robinson, Hyrum Smith and Amasa M. Lyman. On November 1st a court-martial was held, when the prisoners were ordered shot at 8 o'clock the next morning, but General Doniphan protested in the name of humanity, and the sentence was not executed. Instead General Lucas took them on a parade through the neighboring counties.

At the point of the bayonet, the Saints were compelled to sign away their property. Not alone this, but the city was given into the hands of the allied soldiers and marauders who plundered property, and committed horrid, nameless crimes upon the defenceless citizens.

General Clark appeared upon the scene on the 4th of November, approving all that had been done. Calling a mass meeting, he read to the Saints his famous address, in which he referred to the Governor's exterminating order and his determination to see that it was executed, declared that the Saints must leave, and that they need never expect to see the faces of their leaders again "for their doom is sealed."* He then ordered fifty additional

---

* For a copy of the document see "Autobiography of Parley P. Pratt," p. 225; also Whitney's Utah, p. 162, Vol. 1.

men to be taken prisoners, all of whom were shortly thereafter liberated. Joseph Smith and his brother Hyrum, Sidney Rigdon, Lyman Wight, Parley P. Pratt and a few others were committed to jail, as a result of the trial in Richmond, the charges against them being murder, arson, treason, in addition to nearly all other crimes on the calendar.* It was impossible for their friends to do anything to assist them owing to the existing prejudice. Their attorney, General Doniphan, had said: "Offer no defense; for if a cohort of angels should declare your innocence it would be all the same. The judge is determined to throw you into prison."

While the trial lasted from the 11th to the 28th of November, in prison they were compelled to listen for days and nights to the vile stories of the guards, who delighted to taunt them with repetitions of the murders and rapes committed in Far West. One night the Prophet arose, after hearing all he could endure of these filthy tales; in his chains he stood erect in terrible majesty, and in a voice of thunder rebuked the quailing guards who, crouching at his feet with weapons on the ground, begged his pardon, and were silent.†

Elder Rigdon was at length released on bail, and forced to flee for his life, while Joseph, Hyrum, Lyman Wight, Alexander McRae and Caleb Baldwin were removed to Liberty jail, Clay County (the others remaining

---

* "One evidence of their treason, as cited in open court, was their avowed belief in the prophecy of Daniel—chapters II and VII—relative to the setting up of the latter day kingdom of God. Their murders were the battles and skirmishes they had had with the mob. The depredations and deeds of blood committed by the Missourians against the Mormons apparently cut no figure in the case."—Whitney's Utah, Vol. 1, p. 163.

† "Autobiography of Parley P. Pratt," p. 229.

at Richmond), where they spent the winter of 1838-9. It was in this jail that Joseph wrote the interesting prophecies and instructions recorded in Sections 121, 122, and 123 of the Doctrine and Covenants.

The Saints were left in the hands of the mob, who continued their depredations with increased bitterness, destroying property, burning houses, driving off stock, and insulting defenceless women.

It did not seem possible that a community convicted of no crime should be permitted to suffer as the Saints had done under the Boggs' order, and under the enforced treaty depriving them of their property, and yet find no redress. So thinking, those among the Mormon leaders who had regained their liberty addressed a memorial to the legislature of Missouri setting forth the wrongs inflicted upon the Saints, praying for a redress of grievances, and that the Governor's unlawful and tyrannical order be rescinded. The only answer was a show of help in a ridiculously small appropriation for their aid, consumed mostly among the distributing officers.

The depredations continuing, it became painfully apparent, in January, 1839, that there was no help for the Mormons. They were told plainly, both publicly and privately that they must leave the state or be killed. Stripped of the accumulations of years of toil, all that they owned gone, careworn, parts of families in prison, many without clothing or the necessities of life, the only prospect before the Saints was a mid-winter exodus, they knew not where.

It was with the Church in this condition that Brigham Young, President of the Twelve, the Prophet in prison, taking his position as leader, planned and carried into effect the exodus of the Saints to Illinois. He and his brethren entered into covenant to "stand by and assist each other to the utmost of our abilities in removing from this state, and that we will never desert the poor, who are worthy, till they shall be out of the reach of the exterminating order of General Clark, acting for and in the name of the state." It was faithfully kept by them and by the hundreds of others who signed it.

"That winter from ten to twelve thousand Latter-day Saints," says Whitney, "men, women and children, still hounded and pursued by their merciless oppressors, fled from Missouri, leaving in places their bloody footprints on the snow of their frozen pathway. Crossing the icy Mississippi they cast themselves, homeless, plundered and penniless, upon the hospitable shores of Illinois. There their pitiable condition and the tragic story of their wrongs awoke widespread sympathy and compassion, with corresponding sentiments of indignation and abhorrence toward their persecutors."

Cheering them from his dungeon cell, the Prophet wrote: "Zion shall yet live though she seemeth to be dead."

Escaping from Missouri by the tacit permission of their drunken guards, Joseph and Hyrum joined their families at Quincy, Illinois, on the 22nd day of April, 1839. As in other parts of the state, the citizens of Quincy had extended sympathy and welcome to the unfortunate Saints who were made to feel that they were in a place of refuge, temporary though it might be. Thousands of dollars, clothing and provisions, were donated to them by the citizens of Illinois; and while there were doubtless enemies, every popular sentiment both in that state and in Iowa, was in favor of granting them peace and protection. The Governors of both states were their friends. Two days after his arrival, it was decided by a council that Joseph, Vinson Knight and Alonzo Ripley should proceed to select a location for the Church. Already the Mormon leaders, by the written counsel of the Prophet, had made arrangements for land in the two states. Tracts had been purchased in Keokuk, Iowa, forty miles above Quincy; also in Nashville, six miles above Keokuk, and in Montrose, Iowa, four miles above the latter place. Opposite Montrose, just across the river, on the Illinois side, stood Commerce, where Daniel H. Wells resided, of whom the Saints received land on very cheap terms. On the 1st day of May, Joseph made additional purchases in Commerce, and decided to locate the headquarters of the Church there. Arriving with his family on the 10th of May, he took up his abode in a small log cabin on the banks of the river. The village was an insignificant place with only six houses. Marshy, and covered with trees and brush, it had an unhealthy climate, and was a fit abiding place for malarial diseases. On this account the New York company who had started the place were glad to sell when the Mormon agents came. But the city's location was beautiful, overlooking as it did the almost encircling Mississippi. Because of the loveliness of its position, the city was rechristened, and the following year named Nauvoo, signifying beauty and rest.

It was a marvelous undertaking to gather the scattered, destitute and afflicted people, against whom Missouri had committed such a monstrous crime, and establish them in one spot; especially does it so appear when it is remembered that the region around that spot was so sickly that few others could endure its climate. But as in following years, they were assured that the waste desert should blossom at their bidding, so now the Saints were given to understand that the blessing of God would make their present location a fit habitation for them. On this assurance, in their poverty and affliction, they trustingly proceeded to build their homes anew. But at first they were balked by the deadly fevers. Scarcely a family was exempt from sickness. The Prophet himself was prostrated, but the Spirit of God rested powerfully upon him, and on the 22nd day of July he arose and went about administering to the sick, commanding them in the name of the Lord Jesus Christ to arise and be made whole. Many wonderful instances of healing are recorded as a result of the faith of that day of miracles.*

On account of the ravages of disease, and the labors connected with the movement of the Saints, the Twelve had not yet departed on their missions "across the great waters," to which they had been called by revelation the year previous, in Missouri. But they had taken leave of their brethren and the city, on the Temple grounds at Far West, on April 26th, 1839, as it had been declared by the Prophet the year previous that they should. Having learned of this prophecy, Captain Bogart determined it should not be fulfilled, which doubtless accounts for his cruelty in driving out of the state the few remaining Mormons, whom he expelled about the middle of April. Evidently he desired to make it impossible for them to fulfill the revelation, but at 1 o'clock a.m. on the day named in the revelation, seven of the Twelve met, held a conference, laid a corner stone of the tem-

---

* See Cannon's Life of Joseph Smith, p. 293.

ple, ordained Wilford Woodruff and George A. Smith to the Apostleship, severed thirty-one persons from the Church, bade adieu to the city and the remaining Saints, and were on their way to Illinois before their enemies had arisen to renew their oath that the words of the Prophet should go unfulfilled.

During the summer and fall of 1839, Commerce arose like a fairy from the marshes. It became a healthful and charming abiding place. The Saints prospered marvelously in temporal affairs, while their spiritual interests were nourished by the wise counsels of the Prophet and his associates. Through their teachings many sincere souls believed and joined the Church.

In August and September of this year, seven of the Twelve Apostles left for England to fill their missions notwithstanding a number of them and their families were still suffering from the effects of sickness. While abroad they were greatly prospered and the great missionary work begun by Heber C. Kimball and his associates received fresh impetus by their arrival in Liverpool on the 6th of April, 1840. The *Millennial Star* was established, five thousand copies of the Book of Mormon were printed, besides three thousand hymn books and fifty thousand tracts. The first emigrants, numbering over one thousand souls, were forwarded to the Zion of the new world, thus adding a new significance to the doctrine of the gathering. A permanent shipping agency was established, while over three thousand souls were added to the believers. President Brigham Young, who had supervised this work, returned to Nauvoo with some of his brethren, on the first day of July, 1841.

In the meantime the Prophet, soon after planting his people in their new resting place, had taken steps to lay before the general Government the grievances of the driven Saints. On the 29th of October, 1839, he left for Washington on this business, arriving there, with his companion, Judge Elias Higbee, on the 28th of November. Presenting themselves at the White House the following day, they laid before President Van Buren the claims of the Saints against the state of Missouri. He was at first averse to having anything to do with them, remarking, "What can I do? I can do nothing for you. If I do anything I shall come in contact with the whole state of Missouri." But they insisted on a hearing, and the President afterward modified his words, expressing sympathy for the afflicted people, also a desire to hear an exposition of the Prophet's religious views. Joseph explained the gospel to him, and bore a faithful testimony to the work of God. But at a subsequent visit, the President treated him with insolence, and after listening impatiently to his story made that remarkable, now notorious, reply: "Your cause is just, but I can do nothing for you; and if I take up for you, I shall lose the vote of Missouri." Little wonder that the Prophet concluded that the President was "an office seeker, that self-aggrandizement was his ruling passion, and that justice and righteousness were no part of his composition."

Joseph remained in the East during the winter, making the acquaintance of many of the leading political lights in the nation. To the tale of the Mormon's persecutions Senator John C. Calhoun remarked: "It involves a nice question—the question of states rights; it will not do to agitate it." A rather strange answer when subsequent events are considered. Henry Clay remarked to the Prophet's story: "You had better go to Oregon," a statement which then meant out of the permanent reach of civilization, exiles from their native country. The members of Congress from Illinois, doubtless out of political policy, (the Mormons would soon hold the balance of power in Illinois), agreed to present a memorial, petition and documents to the Senate, setting forth the sufferings and claims of the Saints. They did so, but there the matter rested. Nothing was ever done, either by the Executive or the Legislative departments of the national Government to call the state of Missouri to account for the cruel wrongs it had inflicted upon the Mormons.*

Disgusted at length with the politicians whose ruling principles, he discovered, were "popular clamor, and personal aggrandizement," instead of the peace and welfare of the whole people, the Prophet left Washington for home, arriving in Nauvoo, March 4th, 1840. While absent, he had taken advantage of many opportunities to preach the gospel, having addressed large audiences in Washington, in Chester County, Pennsylvania, (where he formed the acquaintance of Edward Hunter, afterward presiding Bishop of the Church) and in the city of Philadelphia.

In the meantime the cause was prospering in Nauvoo and the region round about, under the presidency of Hyrum Smith. There was now a population of about three thousand in the city, with three ecclesiastical wards, which soon grew to twenty thousand, with ten wards and three additional in the farming districts on the outside.

At this time the Mormons again began to take an

---

* The claims of 491 persons against Missouri, amounting to about one and one-half million dollars, were presented by the Prophet with the memorial, all of which were referred to the Committee on Judiciary, which finally reported adversely upon them.

active interest in politics—a right which had brought upon them serious troubles in the past, and which was destined to overwhelm them in the near future with untold sorrow; though for the present it was an important element in the peace and prosperity which smiled upon them. Holding the balance of power in Illinois, their favor was widely sought by politicians. They were the means of electing the celebrated Stephen A. Douglass to the Senate. They voted for Wm. Henry Harrison, the successful Whig candidate for the Presidency, against Martin Van Buren, the Democrat, evidently not so much because they or their Prophet were Whigs, as that Van Buren was their enemy.

With politics immediately there arose the dark specter of persecution. On the 15th of September, 1840, Governor Boggs of Missouri made a demand on Governor Carlin of Illinois for the Prophet and some of the leading Elders, on the grounds that they were fugitives from justice. Considerable annoyance was thus caused, especially to Joseph, whose aged father had died the day previous, but the Missourians received but little sympathy, and the requisition papers were returned unserved. The unpleasant incident, however, like a cloud on the clear horizon of Joseph and his people, was the forerunner of "a storm which, though not bursting forth instanter, shall know no lull when once its fury breaks, till the blood of that Prophet has been shed, and another and a crowning exodus of that people—from the confines of civilization to the wilds of the savage west—shall have startled by its strangeness and awakened by its unparalleled achievement, a world's wonder."*

---

*Whitney' Utah, p. 178, Vol. 1.

In the winter of 1840-1, the legislature granted a most liberal charter to Nauvoo, a charter intended, according to Joseph, "for the salvation of the Church, on principles so broad, that every honest man might dwell secure under its protective influence without distinction of sect or party." It went into effect February 1st, 1841, on which day the first election was held. A day or two thereafter, the University and the Nauvoo Legion were organized, as provided in the charter. Joseph was afterward chosen Lieutenant-General of the military organization.

At a conference on the 6th day of April, 1841, the corner stones of the Nauvoo temple were laid, and to aid in the erection of this edifice and other public buildings, the Prophet called upon the people in the scattered stakes in the region round about to gather to Nauvoo. In conformity with this desire, the Saints flocked into the city from all directions to build up, with their concentrated energy and enterprise, "the corner stone of Zion."

Success attended them at home and abroad, and with the return of Brigham Young and the Aposles from England, the prosperity of the growing city was greatly accelerated. The fame of Joseph Smith had spread over two continents. In 1842 he and his people were at the height of prosperity. The great newspapers sent representatives to write about the modern "military Prophet" and his followers whose surroundings had never before been so propitious as at this particular time. In answer to appeals from publishers, Joseph wrote a short account of the founding of the Church, its progress and persecutions, in which is contained the Articles of Faith.*

---

* For a copy, See Cannon's Life of Joseph Smith, pp. 364—370.

Other writings explaining the belief and the history of the Latter-day Saints were scattered broadcast over the whole world. *Times and Seasons*, the Church organ, was edited by the Prophet himself, through which source he promulgated many precious truths, and instructions. On the 17th of March, the Relief Society of the ladies was organized. Hundreds were baptized. Beautiful homes surrounded by lovely gardens sprang into existence; industries flourished with the increase of population; the thrift, energy and union of the people promised to make the city the largest in the state. Nauvoo, the Beautiful, soon numbered twenty thousand souls.

Zion was indeed living; but, standing upon the gilded hill-tops of her fame and prosperity, the Prophet beheld premonitory shadows of the dark valley of affliction through which her people were about to pass, and in which he was to sacrifice his life, a martyr to her wondrous cause.

3. LOWERING CLOUDS.

The premonition of his own fate first found utterance in a funeral sermon which the Prophet delivered over the remains of a son of Joseph Marks, President of the Nauvoo Stake, on the 9th day of April, 1842, in which he enjoined his hearers to remember that he was subject to death, and that he had no longer a lease of his life.* Four months later, on the 6th day of August,

---

* Said he: "Some of the Saints have supposed that 'Brother Joseph' could not die; but this is a mistake. It is true that there have been times when I have had the promise of my life to accomplish certain things; but, having now done these things, I have no longer any lease of my life. I am as liable to die as other men."

in a conversation with some of his brethren in Montrose, Iowa, he foreshadowed the migration of his people to the west, and the tribulations through which they were to pass, in a remarakable prophecy which was recorded at the time.*

In May, 1842, the treachery of Dr. J. C. Bennett began to come 'to light. This man Bennett had been elected Mayor of Nauvoo, chosen Chancellor of its University, and Major-General of its Legion. He was a man of brains and ability, but had little character and conscience. He had, however, rendered valuable service to the Mormon cause in obtaining the charter of Nauvoo, and as his rascality and lack of soul were not at first apparent, he was hastily loaded with the confidence and honor which he afterward so shamefully abused. At a sham battle of the Legion, he planned to have the Prophet killed. Failing in this, he began repeating unwarranted falsehoods against the Prophet and the people. Among other things, he taught secretly to men and women that Joseph countenanced sin between the sexes. This was doubtless done to shield his own iniquity, for he was shortly after excommunicated for adultery. Then he wrote a book full of wicked falsehoods against Joseph and the Saints which greatly increased the now rising prejudice against them. In August, the Apostles and a large number of Elders were sent out to refute these slanders and vile imputations.

---

* Says the record: "I prophesied that the Saints would continue to suffer much affliction, and would be driven to the Rocky Mountains. Many would apostatize, others would be put to death by our persecutors, or lose their lives in consequence of exposure and disease; and some would live to go and assist in making settlements and building cities, and see the Saints become a mighty people in the midst of the Rocky Mountains."

In the meantime the old Missouri feud was kept alive. In May an attempt was made to assassinate Ex-Governor Boggs, in Independence, the deed being, of course falsely, laid to the Mormons. Complaint was made accusing Joseph of being an accessory to the attempted murder before the crime. Application was made by the Governor of Missouri demanding his person from the authorities in Illinois. He and O. P. Rockwell were accordingly arrested at Nauvoo, August 8th, but were discharged after a hearing before the municipal court. But other attempts were made to get him into the clutches of his enemies, and for this reason he deemed it best to go into hiding. While hidden he wrote important letters to the Saints concerning the continuation of work on the temple, and on the doctrine of baptism for the dead.* Every attempt was made to capture him but in vain. In December, 1842, Thomas Ford, a Democrat, became Governor of Illinois, and to him Joseph applied to withdraw the writs and the proclamations of reward which Governor Carlin had issued for his capture. Ford induced him to submit to a judicial investigation, which was accordingly done, and resulted in Joseph once more becoming a free man.

For a short time he enjoyed peace. On February 6th, 1843, he was chosen Mayor of Nauvoo. On the 12th of April following, Parley P. Pratt, Lorenzo Snow and Levi Richards arrived in the city with two large companies of emigrants from England, among whom were the Cannon family.

In June of this year, there was another attempt to drag the Prophet to Missouri, this time on the old

---

*See Doctrine and Covenants, Section 127 and 128.

charge of treason. Dr. Bennett was among the principal instigators of this outrage. The Prophet was arrested, or rather kidnapped, and brutally treated, but upon a final hearing was again released.

The politicians were stirring up strife against the Saints, in the mean time. Ford in his inaugural address to the legislature had recommended a modification and restriction of the Nauvoo charter, to pacify the general clamor. The step Joseph had taken in calling the Saints from other parts to Nauvoo, previously referred to, had been looked upon as a deep scheme on his part to gain political ascendency, and certain politicians professed to view with alarm the increase of Mormon power which would be brought about by means of this concentration. The result had been the organization of the anti-Mormon party, which was composed of all kinds of people who had grievances against the Saints, and it was the means of stirring up much bitterness against them. In August, several Mormons who had been elected to county offices, upon attempting to qualify at Carthage, the county seat, were threatened by an armed mob, but nevertheless they took the required oaths. With this the anti-Moromn party renewed their pledges to fight the Mormons and assist Missouri in any future attempt to harass the Prophet. Besides this, mobs now began to burn the homes of the Saints in the districts lying outside of Nauvoo, and otherwise to destroy their possessions. When appealed to for assistance, Governor Ford implied in his reply that the Saints must protect themselves. His answer was in the same line as those of former officials in Missouri, and as that of President Van Buren; it meant to that persecuted people:

however just your cause, we can do nothing for you.

The Nauvoo Legion was held in readiness to protect the people from the depredations of the mob.

---

4. THE MARTYRDOM.

"What will be your rule of action relative to us as a people, should fortune favor your ascension to the chief magistracy?"

This question was directed to several prominent national politcians by the Prophet Joseph in the winter of 1843-4. Replies were received from Henry Clay and John C. Calhoun only, and these were so evasive that the Prophet stingingly reproved them for what he considered their cowardice and lack of moral force.

Then followed the startling announcement that Joseph Smith was a candidate for the Presidency of the United States. He was nominated on the 29th of January, 1844, and duly sustained at a state convention on the 17th of May following. Subsequently appeared a printed proclamation of the Prophet's "Views on the Powers and Policy of the Government of the United States," in which he defined his position on the burning political questions of the day. Slavery should be abolished, the slave-holders to be paid for their slaves by the general government; money for this purpose to be raised by the reduction of salaries of Congressmen, and by the sale of public lands. The abolition of imprisonment for debt, and for all crimes save murder, work on public improvements to be made the penalty for others; the penitentiaries to be turned into seminaries of learning. The investment of power in the President to send armies to suppress mobs. The extension of the United States, with the consent of the red man, from sea to sea. The annexation of Texas, and other districts when they should ask for entrance into the Union. Besides there were many other excellent features in his platform.

To promulgate his political views and to act as his electioneers in the campaign, the Twelve and many Elders were sent to the Eastern States. The reason impelling him to accept the candidacy was that he might battle for the religious and civil rights of his people.* Doubtless he had little faith in winning the race for the Presidency. Said he: "I care but little about the Presidential chair, I would not give half as much for the office of President of the United States, as I would for the one I now hold as Lieutenant-General of the Nauvoo Legion."

We find him more interested in having Oregon and California explored, whither, after the completion of the temple, he hoped to lead his Legion at the head of the Saints, there to "build a city in a day." The exploring expedition of seventy-five men which he had arranged for would have gone on this mission but for the political move referred to. In March, Congress was memorialized by him to pass an act for the protection of American citizens wishing to settle Oregon, which at that time was claimed by England jointly with the United States. He asked for the privilege of raising 100,000 men for this purpose, and also to protect Texas against Mexico, and to found another state for the Union in the midst of the

---

*"I feel it to be my right and privilege to obtain what influence and power I can, lawfully, in the United States, for the protection of injured innocence; and if I lose my life in a good cause, I am willing to be sacrificed on the altar of virtue, righteousness and truth, in maintaining the laws and constitution of the United States, if need be for the general good of mankind."
—Joseph Smith.

Rocky Mountains. But other events intervened to prevent him from accomplishing the plan. However, the design was not defeated. Joseph was destined to die, and Brigham Young to carry into effect the outlined program.

The situation in Nauvoo during the spring and summer of 1844 was desperate. Not only were there dire threatenings from the mob without, but from apostates within, who were forming all kinds of plots for the destruction of the Prophet and the people in the fated city. William and Wilson Law, the Higbees, and the Fosters, all of them apostates, and as vile as they were bitter, were foremost among the plotters. These men founded a new church, with William Law, formerly Joseph's counselor, as president, and denounced Joseph as "a fallen Prophet."

The doctrine of plurality of wives and the eternity of the marriage covenant had been recorded July 12th, 1843,* and at the time of which we write was secretly taught and practiced among the leaders of the Church. Owing to his position, William Law, of course, knew this, and therefore had Joseph arrested for polygamy. He was discharged, but it was not him alone that the efforts of these apostates were directed against; the whole people were to be harrassed and persecuted. To this end they founded the *Expositor*, a newspaper whose mission, among other things, was to advocate the unconditional repeal of the Nauvoo charter, and to create disobedience, and rebellion against the Prophet. It made its first appearance June 7th, 1844, filled with foul

---

* Doctrine and Covenants, Section 132.

abuse and filthy scandals. The whole city was shocked. The city council met on the 10th, and dec ared the paper a nuisance that must be abated, and on the day following, by order of Mayor Joseph Smith, it was utterly destroyed. Immediately leaving the city, the proprietors arranged for the arrest of Jseph and a number of prominent men on the charge of riot. They were arrested, tried, and discharged in Nauvoo, they being unwilling to leave that city for trial. This caused intense excitement. Soon anti-Mormon mobs gathered against Nauvoo armed for battle, swearing vengeance on the people and their leaders. The situation was serious. Word had been sent to the Governor, but there had been no reply from him. Under these circumstances Joseph, seeing no escape from threatened assault and massacre, declared Nauvoo under martial law, calling out the Legion to defend it. Hearing of this the weak and vacillating Governor Ford placed himself at the head of the troops, virtually transforming the assembling mobs into militia, demanded that the Prophet and his associates in the destruction of the *Expositor* come to Carthage for trial, and that martial law be abolished in Nauvoo. His orders were obeyed. He made a solemn pledge upon his honor and the faith of the state of Illinois that the prisoners should be protected from violence and that they should be given a fair trial. This pledge was repeated several times afterward, but was never kept.

On the day following, by demand of the Governor, the Legion delivered up their arms, being once more promised protection. The Prophet, his brother Hyrum, and sixteen others of their friends went to Carthage on the evening of the 24th of June, Joseph remarking that he was going "like a lamb to the slaughter."* He had hesitated for a moment, crossed the river with some of his friends thinking to go to the mountains, but returned upon the solicitation of some of his followers who chided him with cowardice in deserting his people. That they were going back to be slaughtered was certain. Their enemies were determined that if the law could not reach them powder and ball should.

On the fatal 27th of June, Joseph and Hyrum, with their friends John Taylor and Willard Richards were placed in an upper room of the Carthage jail. About 5 o'clock p.m. the prophet and his Patriarch brother were shot by a mob of troops about two hundred strong. John Taylor was all but fatally wounded, while Willard Richards escaped unhurt.

While this bloody tragedy was being enacted in Carthage by the mutinous Carthage Greys, Governor Ford was in Nauvoo haranguing the disarmed, peaceful Saints on the enormity of their crimes in destroying the *Expositor*. He must have known of the intention of the mob, for his attention was frequently called to the threats which they had openly made never to allow the Prophet to escape alive. He was "struck with a kind of dumbness," as he heard of the assassination, but it was more from a fear for his own safety than from grief at the crime. He fled to Quincy that same night, after having written an order to the Saints to defend themselves. The horrified mob and citizens of Carthage fled in all directions.

---

* "I am going like a lamb to the slaughter, but I am calm as a summer morning. I have a conscience void of offence toward God and toward all men. If they take my life, I shall die an innocent man, and my blood shall cry from the ground for vengeance, and it shall yet be said of me, 'He was murdered in cold blood.'"

IV. THE CHURCH UNDER BRIGHAM YOUNG.
1844—1877.

1. AGREEMENT TO LEAVE NAUVOO.

The foundation for the Church of Christ, which the Prophet Joseph had laid, was broad and grand. To follow him, God had provided in Brigham Young a strong builder who thoroughly understood the plans and specifications of the complex and colossal superstructure that was thereupon to be erected. With master mind and hand, he stood ready at the appointed hour to grapple with the stupendous task.

The woe and grief of the stricken Saints were beyond description. When the dead bodies of their martyred leaders arrived in Nauvoo, on June 28th, 1844, ten thousand sorrowing people gathered to gaze upon the lifeless clay. Apostle Willard Richards and Col. Markham admonished the people to keep the peace, to look to the law for a remedy, and, that failing, as it did, to leave vengeance to Heaven.

A few days before the martyrdom, the Apostles had been called home from their electioneering mission, but the most of them did not return until the 6th of August.

The training to which the Prophet had subjected the Apostles abundantly fitted them to take the responsibility of leading the Church. His last days had been devoted assiduously to the ministry. He had bestowed upon the Apostles and other faithful Elders, the endowments, given them the keys of the Priesthood in their fullness, taught and administered to them the sealing ordinances, explaining the manner in which parents, children, the whole human family, are to be united in eternal ties. In his sermons he dwelt upon these important doctrines, and laid a foundation broad and strong upon which to build the Church—both relating to government and to spiritual doctrines.* His days had been few but important. All his years were full of persecution; vindictive Hate followed him through life. By "false brethren" he was constantly wounded. He had now sealed his divine doctrines and his faithful testimony with his blood, which, as with other martyrs, became "the seed of the Church."

For the first time since that quorum's organization, the Church was without a First Presidency. But the keys and the powers had been left with the Apostles. Well for the cause that such a character as Brigham Young stood at the head of that quorum. To him the Saints turned instinctively for counsel. Sidney Rigdon, the martyred Prophet's First Counselor, who had removed to Pennsylvania to escape the turmoils of Nauvoo, made an effort to induce the Saints to accept his leadership, but the hearts of the people were not with him; and, after some meetings and discussions, on the 8th of August, 1844, Brigham Young and the Twelve Apostles were sustained as the leaders of the Church. Brigham was regarded by the people as the divinely appointed successor of the Prophet, upon him the mantle of Joseph had fallen. His ability and past labors entitled him to

---

* See Doctrine and Covenants, Section 129-131; also "Sermons and Writings of the Prophet Joseph," *Contributor*, Vol. 111.

their confidence, as the Spirit of God and the gospel designated him their safest guide.* He laid hold of the work where the Prophet finished, and carried it on successfully. It was soon manifest to the enemies of the Church, who paused to view the effects of the murder storm of Carthage, that Mormonism would not die with its Prophet. There had arisen an equally fitting character, however they may have differed, to lead the Saints on their thorny though triumphant way. Upon the foundations laid by the first, the second was to build a structure that was to become the wonder and the admiration of the world.

For a short period there was peace in Nauvoo. The building of the temple and other public places was continued in the midst of poverty. The population was increased by emigrations from the old world. But the enemies of the cause were as active as ever; nothing but the scattering and utter destruction of the Saints would satisfy their designs. Realizing that the enforced and foreshadowed exodus to the west was near at hand, the people were counseled by their leaders to bend every energy to complete the sacred temple, so that all might enjoy the blessings of the glorious doctrines which the martyred Prophet had revealed to them. Before their

---

* "Brigham found himself in possession of qualities which we find present primarily in all great men—intellectual force, mental superiority, united with personal magnetism, and physique enough to give weight to will and opinion; for Brigham Young was assuredly a great man, if by greatness we mean one who is superior to others in strength and skill, moral, intellectual, or physical."—Bancroft's Utah, p. 201.

"A notable character in life's grand tragedy, one bloody scene of which had so lately closed, waiting at the wing he had caught his cue, and the stirring stage of Time was now ready for his advent."—Whitney's Utah, p. 235. Vol. 1.

departure to the west, the edifice was so far completed, that in December, 1845, and January, 1846, thousands received their endowments, blessings and anointings therein.

A faint effort was made in the fall of 1844, also in May, 1845, to bring the murderers of the Prophets to justice, but after a trial, they were "honorably acquitted." There was no hope for the Saints to receive justice. Yielding to the popular clamor, the legislature repealed the Nauvoo city charter, in January, 1845, and the place became the prey of lawlessness.* In April, Governor Ford wrote to President Young advising him to go west with his people, to "get off by yourselves" where "you may enjoy peace."† This course had long been decided upon, and the desire to complete the temple was all that delayed the Saints in carrying out their plans.

In the fall of 1845, encouraged by the acquittal of the fiends of Carthage, mobs became more and more bold in their depredations; outrages, burnings and persecutions were inflicted afresh upon the defenseless Saints. Their houses fired and their possessions destroyed, they fled from the outlying districts to Nauvoo for protection.‡ At this juncture Governor Ford called out the troops to

---

* Said Josiah Lamborn, Esq., Attorney-General of Illinois: "By the repeal of your charter, and by refusing all amendments and modifications our legislature has given a kind of sanction to the barbarous manner in which you have been treated It is truly a melancholy spectacle to witness the lawmakers of a sovereign state condescending to pander to the vices, ignorance and malevolence of a class of people who are at all times ready for riot, murder and rebellion."

† For a copy of this letter, and other documents relating to the departure of the Saints from Nauvoo, see Tullidge's History of Salt Lake City, pp. 8—13.

‡ "Mobs commenced driving out the Mormons in the lower part of Hancock County, and burning their houses and property.—The burning was

restore order. Peace was proclaimed to the people, and the mob was commanded to obey authority. Then, on the 1st of October, was held a conference of the Mormon leaders and General Harding, commander of the troops, with Attorney-General McDougal, Senator Douglass, and Major Warren. The result was an agreement by the Mormons, who well knew that there was no alternative between exodus and extermination by massacre, to leave the state in the spring. On the other hand, they were not to be molested by the mob, but this part was not kept. Their removal had been demanded by a meeting of representatives of nine counties of the state, assembled in Carthage.

As rapidly as possible, preparations were made to move west in compliance with the terms of the agreement, and with the decision of the Church leaders. Land was disposed of, leased or exchanged for animals and wagons. Property of all kinds was sold, or left for sale in the hands of trusted agents. So closed the year 1845.

2. EXPELLED FROM ILLINOIS.

After a little less than seven years of troubled rest, during which time wonderful strides in temporal as well as spiritual progress had been made, the Saints, now twenty thousand strong, once more must leave their homes. Driven again from their city, they must now abandon themselves to the mercy of the savages, journey far beyond the borders of civilization.

---

continued from settlement to settlement for ten or eleven days without any resistance whatever."—Wells in Bancroft's Utah.

"The mob said they would drive all into Nauvoo, and all Nauvoo into the Mississippi."—Richards in Bancroft's Utah.

Hundreds of farms, two thousand houses and much personal property, were now offered for sale in and about Nauvoo. Their many public buildings and their glorious and beloved temple, the Saints did not expect to sell, but they called upon all good citizens to aid them in the disposal of their other possessions, giving the men of Illinois to understand, however, that they would not sacrifice or give away their property. But a community who were unwilling to keep their own conditions of the covenant of peace with the Mormons, could not be expected to render pecuniary assistance to the afflicted people. Possessions were therefore sold for a mere nothing. The country was scoured for miles around and property traded at a fearful sacrifice for traveling outfits.

At length, hurried by their enemies, driven almost at the point of the sword, the Saints gathered in large numbers on the east shore of the river, and, on February 4th, 1846, began crossing the water on their way to the West. After that date, the ferries were kept busy day and night until the river froze over, when crossing was continued on the ice. By the middle of the month, a thousand souls, with their effects, had been landed on the Iowa shore. Proceeding, they made their first camp at Sugar Creek, nine miles west into Iowa.* They suffered severely, the ground being snow-covered and the weather bitter cold. Sleeping in tents and wagons, they and

---

*Says Col. Thomas L. Kane: "The people of Iowa have told me that from morning to night they passed westward like an endless procession. They did not seem greatly out of heart, they said; but at the top of every hill, before they disappeared, were to be seen looking back, like banished Moors, on their abandoned homes and the far-seen temple and its glittering spire."

their sick underwent much hardship and affliction both of body and mind, driven as they were by civilized Christians from comfortable homes, and camping now almost in sight of these, on the bleak prairie, in the dead of winter, with no prospects before them but snow, storms, savages, and the untrodden wilderness. Well might the historian Bancroft exclaim: "There is no parallel in the world's history to this migration from Nauvoo."*

On the 15th, they were joined by President Young, the leading spirit of the exodus, who began the temporary organization of the camp. Firmly but kindly he gave laws for the guidance of the "Camps of Israel," enjoining honesty and morality. Innocent amusement and recreation were to be permitted in moderation, as a means of diverting the peoples' minds from their past troubles and present toils and hardships. Having petitioned the Governor for protection while passing through his territory, President Young and the Apostles made a farewell visit to Nauvoo, holding a parting service in the temple where the remnant of the Saints were instructed in their duties. This done, they returned to camp, and on March 1st orders to advance were given. Five miles were covered that day. Then from day to day they continued their journey in rain, snow and mud, towards the setting sun, their hearts cheered by the God of the friendless. Many were poor, some were destitute, but all were as happy as could be under the circumstances. They never uselessly repined, but watched, prayed,

---

* Bancroft's Utah, p. 217.

worked, listened to music, danced, sang and rejoiced.*

At Shoal Creek, near Chariton River, on March 27th, a more complete organization was effected. Captains were appointed over "hundreds," "fifties" and "tens." Reinforced by fresh arrivals, the companies soon numbered about three thousand wagons, thousands of cattle, besides sheep, horses and mules. Settlements sprang up in the wilderness of Iowa as if by magic. They were called "traveling stakes of Zion," and chief among these were Garden Grove and Mount Pisgah, near which farming operations were carried on for the benefit of those who should follow after.

In July the main body reached the Missouri, settling in a place which they named Kanesville, now known as Council Bluffs. President Young and the vanguard had arrived about the middle of June. Later a part of the company crossed the river and settled upon the Pottawatomie and Omaha Indian lands, where Winter Quarters, now Florence, was founded, with a population of about four thousand souls.

It was President Young's intention to hasten on that summer with an exploring party to the Rocky Mountains. The muster for volunteers for this purpose was in progress at Mount Pisgah, under the direction of Apostle Wilford Woodruff, recently returned from England, when a startling incident occurred which changed his plans

---

*"A spectacle sublime. An exiled nation, going forth like Israel from Egypt, into the wilderness, there to worship, unmolested, the God of their fathers in His own appointed way; that from their loins might spring a people nursed in the spirit of prophecy, made stalwart by tribulation, that should leap from the mountains in a day to come, and roll back, an avalanche of power, to regain possession of their promised land."—Whitney's Life of Heber C. Kimball, p. 363.

and delayed the migration west until the following spring. Their country made a call for volunteers for quite another purpose—a requisition for a battalion of five hundred men to take part in the Mexican war. There were now twelve thousand Mormons inhabiting the temporary settlements stretched across the plains of Iowa from Winter Quarters to Garden Grove.

3. TWO MILITARY PICTURES.

Whatever may have been the cause of the Government's requisition for the Mormon Battalion, whether its muster was meant for their good or their evil, whether in answer to their petition for help, or in fulfillment of Senator Benton's threat that they would be destroyed if they failed to comply, certain it is that the Saints viewed it with alarm as the news sped from tent to tent through the "Camps of Israel." They looked upon it as a scheme for their destruction, as a test of their loyalty, which it was feared, in the conditions that surrounded them would result in their annihilation. Think of taking five hundred of the young, able-bodied men, the flower of the camps, from their present all but helpless ranks! Consider the dependent ones that would be left behind in an Indian country, without means of support, in the midst of the dangers and hardships of an unparalleled exodus! Their plight, too, brought about, they considered, by the nation now calling for help! Had it not thrust them from its borders? Had not all their petitions to it for redress been rejected? And now, that nation calling upon them to assist in fighting its battles! Then arose the memories of Missouri, the martyrdom, their recent treatment by the government of Illinois, their present condition! Natural indeed that they should ask, What shall be done? What will our leaders decide to do?

When Captain James Allen, acting under General Kearney, commander of the army of the west, arrived in Council Bluffs, on July 1st, to lay before President Young his errand to muster volunteers, he was promptly told that he should have his men. "You shall have your battalion," said Brigham. The loyalty of the Mormons, their love of country, their devotion to the Union, were the considerations alone that could have insured such a patriotic reply at such a time.

There not being men enough in Winter Quarters, President Young and others proceeded to the various camps in the role of recruiting officers. At Mt. Pisgah many were enrolled. Messengers were sent to other camps and to Nauvoo for young men, old men, and boys to fill the places made vacant by the enlisted men. At Council Bluffs, upon the arrival of the Pisgah volunteers, the enrollment was completed, on the 15th of July. Addressing the Saints at a meeting in the Bowery, President Young cautioned them "not to mention families that day. "We want to conform to the requisition made upon us. We must raise the battalion. I say it is right; and who cares for sacrificing our comfort for a few years?"

The result is thus summarized by Col. Kane who was present at the time: "A central mass meeting for counsel, some harangues at the remotely scattered camps, an American flag brought out from the store-house of things rescued and hoisted to the top of a tree-mast, and in three days the force was reported, mustered, organized and ready to march."

The Battalion, numbering in all five-hundred and forty-nine souls, took up their western march on the 16th, having on the evening previous taken leave of their loved ones, and enjoyed themselves in a social re-union, with music, song and dance. For two thousand miles, from the Missouri to the Pacific, the Battalion marched over dreary deserts, braving dangers and hardships, finally reaching California, January 29th, 1847.* Whatever else may be said of the Mormons, let no man dare, after such a test, to question their patriotism and loyalty.

That is one military picture, in the foreground of which stand forth prominently patriotism and loyalty to country under the most trying circumstances that could be named—an enduring honor to the Mormons.

Now the other.

After the departure of the leaders, in 1846, such haste was made by the remaining Saints to leave Nauvoo as should have been satisfactory to any reasonable person. But the anti-Mormons affected to believe, and freely asserted, that the Mormons did not intend to leave the State.† In July, they raised troops to march against

---

* Says Lieutenant-Col. St. George Cooke, in charge of the Battalion, vice Col. J. Allen, deceased: "History may be searched in vain for an equal march of infantry; nine-tenths of it through a wilderness, where nothing but savages and wild beasts are found; or deserts where, for the want of water, there is no living creature. There, with almost hopeless labor, we have dug deep wells, which the future traveler will enjoy. Without a guide who had traversed them, we have ventured into trackless prairies, where water was not found for several marches. With crow-bar and pick-ax in hand, we have worked our way over mountains which seemed to defy aught save the wild goat, and hewed a passage through a chasm of living rock, more narrow than our wagons."

† "In short, from the first of May to the final evacuation of the city, the men of Illinois never ceased from strife and outrage."—Bancroft's Utah, p. 226.

Nauvoo. The new citizens averted a conflict at that time, but on September 10th and 12th, a mob led by Col. Brockman, a Campbellite preacher, proceeded to bombard the city. The citizens, greatly outnumbered, banded together for defense, but were overpowered, in a conflict, on the 12th, of over an hour's duration, during which several citizens were killed. Then followed a siege of several days, which ended in a treaty whose main provisions were the surrender of the city, the immediate departure of the remaining Mormons (numbering something over 600 souls), the protection of property and persons from violence, and the sick to be treated humanely.

No sooner did the mob get possession of the city, however, than the agreement was outrageously violated by them. The citizens were treated with every indignity, and finally all the Mormons who had not already fled, were forced, at the point of the bayonet, to abandon their homes and possessions. The last remnant crossed the river September 17th. They, and their sick and destitute, were dumped, shelterless, penniless, with scarcely any food or clothing, upon the flats of the western shore of the Mississippi. Their deserted city was pillaged, plundered; its holy temple desecrated with the boisterous orgies and vulgar songs of a drunken mob.

What became of the driven Mormons? "Where were they? They had last been seen, carrying in mournful train their sick and wounded, halt and blind, to disappear behind the western horizon, pursuing the phantom of another home. Hardly anything else was known of them; and people asked with curiosity, what had been their fate—what their fortune."*

---

* From Col. Kane's lecture before the Historical Society of Pennsylvania.

And all this, while their brethren of the Mormon Battalion were marching under the good old flag to do battle for their country's cause, on the plains of Mexico!

That is another military picture, in which the sullied good name of one of the sovereign states of the Union, Illinois, with her weak and wavering Governor, stands prominently in the foreground to their everlasting shame and disgrace.

Most of the twenty thousand population of Nauvoo were now sojourning in the wilderness with the "Camps cf Israel." They endured much suffering. There was a lack of food and clothing. Fevers broke out among them, and many slept the sleep of death on the prairies. At Winter Quarters alone, there were over six hundred buried. Yet with all this, the spirits of the people were kept buoyant with labor and the hope of better days.

In Winter Quarters, nearly seven hundred log and turf houses were erected, the city being laid out with streets in regular order. There were factories, shops, mills, and a tabernacle of worship, the whole being fortified in frontier fashion. Everybody was kept busy, the organizations of the Church were continued, religious meetings held, missionaries sent abroad, schools established. Many scattered through the western states in search of work. Teams and supplies were sent back to relieve the poor remnants of Nauvoo, in their flight from tyrant mobs.

And so passed the winter of 1846-7.

---

4. THE PIONEERS AND FIRST COMPANIES.

On the 14th of January, 1847, President Brigham Young made known "The Word and Will of the Lord

Concerning the Camps of Israel in their Journeyings to the West."* In this manifesto are found the instructions that should guide the Saints in their continued travels. In conformity therewith, they made early preparations to vacate Winter Quarters, and to depart for their unknown inheritances in the wilderness. Twelve times twelve able-bodied men were selected to pave the way.† These pioneers started from Winter Quarters on the 7th of April. On the 8th they encamped near the Elkhorn, and during the next few days following the 17th of April, when the camp was about sixty miles west of the starting point, the members were organized thoroughly into a military company, with Brigham Young as Lieutenant-General, Stephen Markham as Colonel, and fourteen captains.

Prepared and equipped to fight (if necessary), and to construct their way over the rivers, plains and mountains of the thousand-mile journey before them, they continued their westward, pilgrim march for three months and seventeen days. They followed the north bank of the Platte, making a new road for the benefit of those who should come after, for over six hundred miles, and for the remainder of the distance following a trail made by trappers. At length, after many thrilling experiences, on the since celebrated 24th of July, President Young and his band of pioneers entered the Valley of the Great Salt Lake. The deserts and mountains had been penetrated. About the grateful wanderers bathed in the thin,

---

* See Doctrine and Covenants, Section 136.

† One of these, Ellis Eames, fell sick, and returned to camp, leaving the number of the Pioneers at 143, with three women and two children. They had seventy-two wagons, ninety-three horses, fifty-two mules, sixty-six oxen and nineteen cows, besides seventeen dogs and some chickens.

clear air, lay the new land of Zion, the resting-place beheld by their inspired leader when the voice whispered to him: "Here is the place where my people Israel shall pitch their tents." The hills reverberated to their hosannah shouts of praise and joy.*

The 25th being Sunday, they held two religious services, thanking God for their deliverance. Pointing to the ancient prophecies, the speakers maintained that these foretold of their coming: "Oh Zion, that bringest good tidings, get thee up into the high mountains." And, again, God was to "hide his people in the chambers of the mountains," and in the last days was to "establish his house on the tops of the mountains, and exalt it above the hills."

Losing no time, they began early the next day to plant potatoes and grain. Companies were organized to explore the surrounding regions. The tall mountain north of the settlement was scaled, and its summit called Ensign Peak, because it was a suitable place to raise an ensign to the nations. The river, the lake, and the hot springs were visited. On the 28th a spot for a temple was selected, and the general plan of the city decided upon. In the early part of August the Twelve and many of the people renewed their covenants by baptism. Everybody was kept busy. Some were tilling the soil, some cutting and hauling timber, building, making adobes, and otherwise preparing for the Saints who were to follow after and inhabit. All were anxious to do as

---

* In the heart of America they are now upon the border of a new Holy Land, with its Desert and its Dead Sea, its River Jordan, Mount of Olives and Galilee Lake, and a hundred other features of its prototype of Asia.—Bancroft's Utah, p. 258.

much as possible before returning to assist their friends. The pioneers had been re-inforced, soon after their arrival, by one hundred and forty men of the Mormon Battalion detachment, and about one hundred Saints from Mississippi.

At a conference on the 22nd day of August, a Stake of Zion was organized, with Father John Smith as President. At this time the settlement was named Great Salt Lake City, and the surrounding creeks and canyons and the river Jordan were christened. The whole region whose waters flow into the Lake was called the Great Basin.

On the 17th, seventy-one men, mostly of the Battalion, had returned, well organized, to Winter Quarters. Later, August 26th, President Young and a company of one hundred and seven persons, also mostly Battalion men who had families among the Saints, started for Winter Quarters, bidding "a hearty good-by to all who tarry."*

In the track of the pioneers were now moving several companies of Saints—distinguished as the first emigrations. In June these were organized on the Elk Horn, in accordance with the instructions left by President Young. Apostles Parley P. Pratt and John Taylor exercised general supervision of the emigrants, who were directed by the committee appointed for this purpose.

---

*Says Wilford Woodruff: "We have traveled with heavily laden wagons more than a thousand miles, over rough roads, mountains, and canyons, searching out a land, a resting place for the Saints. We have laid out a city two miles square, and built a fort of hewn timber drawn seven miles from the mountains, and of sun-dried bricks and adobes, surrounding ten acres of ground, forty rods of which were covered with block-houses, besides planting about ten acres of corn and vegetables. All this we have done in a single month."

There were all told about 560 wagons, 1553 men, women and children, with about 5000 head of stock. John Young was the general commander, with John Van Cott, marshal. Then there were four captains of hundreds— Daniel Spencer, Edward Hunter, Jedediah M. Grant, Abraham O. Smoot—with sub-captains and divisions of "fifties" and "tens;" also an "artillery company" under General C. C. Rich. Among the many prominent founders of Utah who were along with these camps may be named George Q. Cannon (then a youth of twenty), Eliza R. Snow, John Smith (who had been sustained as President of the Salt Lake Stake), Lorin Farr, the Thatchers, William Hyde, Jacob Gates, William W. Riter, William C. Staines, Jesse N. Smith and Chauncey W. West.

The Saints left the Elk Horn in two companies—on the 18th of June, and on the 4th of July. Their progress was hindered by stampedes, and the loss of cattle; and they had some trouble with the Indians. There were six or seven deaths and a number of births on the journey. Their meetings with the pioneers were occasions of great rejoicings. On the Sweetwater a grand feast was held in honor of President Young, at the instance of Apostle Taylor and Bishop Hunter. Important councils were held at various times, and the Saints, who now learned for the first time where their destination was, were cheered and encouraged by the returning pioneers.

In the latter part of September the companies began arriving in the Valley, and before the middle of October all the trains had reached the journey's end in safety.

Reaching Winter Quarters on the 31st of October, the returning brethren, many of whom had not seen their families since the eventful July 16th, 1846, when they parted with them at their country's call, were warmly greeted by their friends and loved ones.

---

5. MIGRATION OF THE MAIN BODY WEST.

There were now two Stakes of Zion—one on the Missouri, which continued to be the headquarters owing to the presence of President Young and most of the Twelve, and one on the borders of the Great Salt Lake, in the midst of the mountains. A thousand miles apart, cheerful and united, but struggling still with hardships and ever-recurring new difficulties, the Saints spent the winter of 1847-8.

In Winter Quarters they had prospered abundantly. True, there had been some sickness and deaths, but the climate was much improved. On the whole, health, abiding peace and good will prevailed among the faithful inhabitants. In contentment and quiet the winter passed away, preparations being eagerly made for the contemplated migration in the spring.

On the 5th of December, at a council of the Apostles, it was decided to organize the quorum of the First Presidency, vacant since the martyrdom of the Prophet. Brigham Young, the chief Apostle, was then chosen President of the Church of Jesus Christ of Latter-day Saints. The action of the Twelve was ratified at a conference of the Church on the 27th, and on the 8th of October the following year was confirmed by a conference at Great Salt Lake City. The Apostles also issued a general epistle, calling upon the Saints to gather to the new Zion in the mountains, and upon all "presidents, and emperors, and kings, and princes, and nobles and governors, and rulers and judges, and all nations, and kindreds, tongues, and people under the whole heaven, to come and help us to build a house to the name of the God of Jacob, a place of peace, a city of rest, a habitation for the oppressed of every clime."*

The seventeen hundred souls who dwelt in Great Salt Lake City passed through the season enjoying moderate comfort under the circumstances.† The winter was mild with but little snow. On October 3rd, after their arrival, the first stake organization was completed. Father John Smith, president, Charles C. Rich and John Young, counselors. A High Council was also organized. Tarleton Lewis was chosen Bishop. Some of the Battalion men, returning from California, brought wheat, corn, potatoes and garden seeds while more seeds also live stock were subsequently imported by settlers who visited the coast. In the spring, wild sego and parsnip roots, and later thistle tops, constituted the vegetable diet. Their beef had been very poor. Dissecting some of it at one time, Apostle Taylor suggested that the saw be greased to make it work. In some instances skins served in lieu of clothing. Catamounts, wolves, foxes, mice and bed-bugs each contributed to make matters unpleasant for the new settlers.

The most serious plague, however, was yet to come. It was the crickets. Appearing in May and June, 1848, black legions of these pests invaded the fields and gardens, literally sweeping the earth clean wherever they passed. All the efforts of the settlers, who, living upon

---

* See *Millennial Star*, Vol. x, p. 81.
† They dwelt in 423 houses, had 5,133 acres of cultivated land, and 875 acres sown with winter wheat.

sego roots and thistles, fought with the desperation of souls who have starvation staring them in the face, to save their crops were unavailing. There seemed to be no help. The harvest would go, and with it the lives dependent upon it! At this critical time, immense flocks of gulls came from the islands of the lake to feast upon the crickets. All day they ate, gorged, vomited, then feasted again, returning each day until the cricket foe was vanquished. The thankful and astonished settlers looked on in wonder, praising God that through a manifestation of His providence they were saved! It is not strange that to this day the gull is a sacred bird among the Saints. In memory of their service to the undaunted pioneer, let there be emblazoned upon the armorial ensign of the new State of Utah the gull and the sego lily.

On the 10th day of August the settlers celebrated their first harvest home. "Large sheaves of wheat," says Parley P. Pratt, "rye, barley, oats and other productions were hoisted on poles for public exhibition, and there was prayer and thanksgiving, congratulations, songs, speeches, music, dancing, smiling faces and merry hearts. Some of the Battalion men, who had remained at work in California returning, increased the population to about 1800 souls. They were among the first to discover the gold fields which were soon to set aflame the civilized world. Some of the dust they brought with them to the valley.

Turning now to the Missouri, we find that early in 1848 active operations were engaged in to migrate the main body of the Church to the mountains. Winter Quarters would shortly be vacated. Desiring an outfitting post in the East, the Mormon leaders petitioned the legislature of Iowa for the organization of Pottawatomie

County, and built the town of Kanesville, east of the river a few miles above the present city of Council Bluffs. At this place for several years the Mormon emigrations were equipped for their journeys over the plains. Coming from Europe, they sailed up the rivers from New Orleans. The first river-route company came under direction of Apostle Franklin D. Richards, landing in Winter Quarters a short time before the first company of that year started for the mountains.

In preparation of the approaching departure, on Sunday, May 14th, President Young publicly pronounced blessings upon those who were going with him to the valley, as well as upon those who were to remain. On this occasion he prophesied that the Saints would never be driven from the Rocky Mountains. On the 24th he led out for the Elk Horn, where the companies were thoroughly organized.* They began their westward travels about the beginning of June. There were three companies -Brigham Young, who had general command of all of them (Daniel H. Wells, his aide-de-camp, and H. S. Eldredge, marshal) came first with 1229 souls, and 397 wagons; Heber C. Kimball, with 662 souls and 226 wagons; Willard Richards, with 526 souls and 169 wagons.† When the last wagon left on the 3rd of July,

---

* "To those who met them on the route, the strict order of their march their coolness and rapidity in closing ranks to repel assaults, their method in posting sentries around camp and corral, suggested rather the movements of a well-organized army than the migration of a people, and in truth, few armies have been better organized or more ably led than was this army of the Lord "—Bancroft's Utah, p. 284.

† There were besides in all the companies: 2012 oxen, 983 cows, 131 horses, 116 mules, 654 sheep, 384 loose cattle, 337 pigs, 904 chickens, 134 dogs, 54 cats, 3 goats, 10 geese, 5 ducks, 11 doves, 1 squirrel, and 5 hives of bees.

Winter Quarters was almost deserted. With this emigration were such famous men in Utah history as Lorenzo Snow, Franklin D. Richards, Joseph F. Smith, Newel K. Whitney, Robert T. Burton, Hosea Stout, and many others. Several of the Apostles who were to go on missions remained in Kanesville, where, on February 7th, 1849, Orson Hyde began the publication of the *Frontier Guardian*.

The companies all followed in the route of the Pioneers. President Young arrived in Great Salt Lake City on the 20th of September, 1848, and within a month all the trains had safely entered the valley. Their presence swelled the population to 5000 souls.

The Church was now in the "Great American Desert," led thither under the inspired direction of Brigham Young, one of the greatest colonizers our country has ever known. It was a desolate abiding place, shunned by all who passed because of its sterility. It was the most inhospitable and forbidding portion of the vast western region of which the great statesman, Daniel Webster, said: "What do we want with this vast, worthless area? This region of savages and wild beasts, of deserts, of shifting sands and whirlwinds of dust, of cactus and prairie dogs? To what use could we ever hope to put these great deserts, or those endless mountain ranges, impenetrable, and covered to their very base with eternal snow?"

Yet in the heart of this domain, the exiled Mormons chose to build their homes. They loved it because of its liberty, because of the freedom that encircled them. By arduous toil and the blessings of God they have built their scores of thrifty cities, subdued the sandy desert, made a garden of the wilderness.

6. COLONIZATION.

To obtain pasturage for their stock, several of the pioneers, soon after their arrival, pressed north founding the settlements in what is now Davis County.* These new places continued to thrive, and before the close of 1848, there were colonies near the present Bountiful, Kaysville, Farmington, and in other places. In January of that year, Captain James Brown purchased the Miles Goodyear claim which included the present site of Ogden City, and the greater portion of Weber County.

These movements to occupy the land were made agreeable to the instructions of President Young, and were a part of his grand scheme to colonize the mountain region with his people. Upon his arrival, in September, 1848, this matter was uppermost in his mind, but he found that the first great question to be solved was the short supply of food. The crops were not so abundant that there would be sufficient for the now increased population. The new companies had brought only little with them. As a result, before a new harvest, there was great scarcity of food, much privation and suffering among the people, which, however, were materially alleviated by the spirit of kindness, oneness and helpfulness that prevailed.† In community fashion, the needy were helped by those who had supplies. To add to their misfortunes, the winter of 1848-9 was very severe.

---

* So named after Captain D. C. Davis of the Mormon Battalion, who settled near the present site of Farmington.

† "Roots had to be dug from the ground for food, raw hides were torn down from roofs, cut into shreds and cooked. Very little game was found, near the city: some fish were obtained."—*Contributor*, Vol. 2, p. 176.

It was while the people were thus distressed that Heber C. Kimball prophesied that within three years "States goods" would be sold cheaper in Salt Lake Valley than in New York. His prophetic utterance found remarkable fulfillment when the adventurous gold hunters from all parts of the earth made Salt Lake their "half-way house," leaving their merchandise, provisions and implements, with the destitute settlers in exchange for animals to carry them more hurriedly to their destination. This was in 1849, and when the settlers grandly celebrated the second anniversary of their arrival into the Valley, the prophecy uttered the year previous was being fulfilled. At the grand feast hundreds of west bound emigrants dined with the happy Mormons. But even this manifestation of divine provision was not enough to prevent some of the Saints from contracting the gold fever. It took the best efforts and the wisest judgment of their leaders to intercept the threatened general migration to the golden west, which would have been then as great a calamity as could have befallen the Church.

The people were stirred to activity. In the fall of 1848, five thousand acres of land were plotted for fencing and cultivation, over eight hundred were sowed in winter wheat. The council house was projected, roads were constructed, grist and saw mills were erected, bridges built, and a proposition was made to bring the waters of the Big Cottonwood to the city. Lots were distributed to the settlers some of whom, moving out of the "Fort," settled upon these. To obviate the inconvenience of a lack of circulating medium, pending the procuring of a stamp to coin the gold dust brought by the Battalion men, a paper currency was issued in January, 1849. Fify-cent and one-dollar bills, upon which the first printing in the Valley was done, were stamped; and a resolution was passed placing certain Kirtland Bank bills in circulation, thus making these notes as good as gold, in fulfillment of a prophecy to that effect by the Prophet Joseph. Later the gold dust was coined into $2.50, $5, $10, and $20 pieces which were used until superceded by legal tender when they were disposed of as bullion to the federal mints.

Keeping constantly in view their religious duties in the midst of their temporal labors, the organizations of the Church were never neglected. On February 12th, 1849, the quorum of Twelve was filled by the calling and ordination of Charles C. Rich, Lorenzo Snow, Erastus Snow and Franklin D. Richards to the Apostleship. A permanent Stake organization was also perfected, and the city was divided into nineteen ecclesiastical wards with a bishop over each. The gathering was not forgotten. In 1849 there were about thirty thousand Saints in Great Britain, ten thousand of whom had joined the Church in the past fifteen months. To assist in redeeming the country, as well as to carry out the commands of God, it was desirable that these should be brought to the mountains. For the purpose of aiding the poor among them to migrate, the Perpetual Emigrating Fund was established in October. A large sum of money was obtained for this fund which was kept in operation thereafter for upwards of forty years, and was the means of assisting thousands to emigrate from the poverty of the Old World to the better surroundings of the New. Bishop Edward Hunter was sent to the frontier to put its provisions into operation, and to take charge of the next season's emigration. At the same time many prominent Elders were called to go to various parts of the earth on missions. They opened the gospel door to France, Scandinavia, Italy, Lower California, and the Society Islands, or were sent to other regions to continue the work of promulgation. The first company brought across the plains by the Emigrating Company arrived in Salt Lake on the 13th of October, 1850.

Colonization continued. What is now Utah, Sanpete, and Tooele Counties, were explored and settled, also Sevier, Iron and other southern counties. Later followed exploring parties and colonies to all parts of the Territory. In each of these the various crafts were represented. They provided themselves with plenty of provisions, stocks, implements and other necessaries. They were generally composed of volunteers, and were sent out by the great colonizer, Brigham Young, under proper ecclesiastical organization. Until the introduction of a regular civil government, the Church officers held secular or temporal administration over the people. The public labors were performed under their direction, they were the judges among the people, and under their supervision and advice went on the great work of founding and building cities, of redeeming the desert. Marvelous indeed are the labors of these empire founders. At present they and their children occupy the country extending for over a thousand miles from Mexico to Canada, and their numerous thrifty cities and villages are found in the valleys of the mountains in nearly every State and Territory of the mighty West. The Saints are the remnants of Israel gathered out from the coasts of the earth, and truly God hath wrought through them "a marvelous work and a wonder."

7. UTAH TERRITORY ORGANIZED.

Up to the spring of 1849, when the political history of Utah properly begins, the settlers had been governed exclusively by the excellent ecclesiastical organizations. There had been little need and less time for civil government, but as emigrants of other faiths began to come into their midst, there was a desire among the leaders of the people to come in under the folds of the Union, as indeed there had been from the beginning, notwithstanding they had been driven by that nation to a foreign country.

By the treaty of Guadalupe Hidalgo, signed February 2nd, 1848, the United States had come into the possession of the vast western region from which was afterward formed the States and Territories of California, Nevada, Utah, New Mexico, and Arizona. The Mormons were well nigh the only occupants of the new domain, and they were hopeful and energetic enough to believe that in time they could subdue and occupy the country which they had assisted in wresting from Mexico, and opened up to civilization.

With a view of introducing civil government to this area, early in March, 1849, a convention was called of "all the citizens of that part of Upper California lying east of the Sierra Nevada Mountains, to take into consideration the propriety of organizing a territorial or state government." This convention assembled in Salt Lake City on the 4th of March. A memorial, signed by Brigham Young and 2,270 others, was sent to Congress, as a result of this convention, April 30th, asking for a "territorial government of the most liberal construction authorized by our most excellent federal constitution, with the least possible delay," which was carried to Washington by Dr. J. M. Bernhisel.

At the convention, a committee was also selected to draft a constitution under which the people might govern themselves, until Congress should take action and otherwise provide by law. On the 10th of March the constitution was adopted and a Provisional Government was organized under the name of the State of Deseret. A legislature, or General Assembly of the State of Deseret, consisting of Senate and House of Representatives, was also elected with powers and duties defined. Brigham Young was elected Governor.* Under this form of government, purely Mormon and not yet sanctioned by the authority of Congress, the new State was governed for nearly two years. Justice was equitably administered to all—both non-Mormon and Mormon, and the decisions of the courts, constantly appealed to by passing emigrants, were remarkable for fairness and impartiality.†

On July 2nd, 1849, the General Assembly of Deseret met at Salt Lake City, and by joint agreement of its two houses, it was decided to pray for the admission of Deseret as a state of the Union. A new memorial was consequently then prepared. Almon W. Babbit was elected delegate to Congress, and was sent to Washing-

---

* Willard Richards, secretary; Horace S. Eldredge, marshal; Daniel H. Wells, attorney-general; besides an assessor and collector, a treasurer, and supervisor of roads; also three judges, Heber C. Kimball, chief justice, and John Taylor and Newel K. Whitney, associates. The bishops of the several wards were elected as magistrates.

† So testifies Captain Howard Stansbury of the U. S. Army Corps of Topographical Engineers who came to Salt Lake City on the 28th of August, 1849, wintered there, and remained with his expedition in the Territory for a whole year, exploring and surveying the Valley of the Great Salt Lake, also Utah Lake and its vicinity, also a route from the Valley to Fort Hall. His widely circulated report to the Government is authority throughout the world in relation to Utah and the people who reclaimed it from a desert.

ton, bearing the memorial and the constitution of the proposed state. Mr. Babbit presented his documents to Congress, with his credentials as delegate from the Provisional State of Deseret, through Senator Stephen A. Douglass, on the 27th of December of that year; but his petition was denied, and he was, of course, not admitted to Congress. Instead, after a delay of nine months, Congress passed a bill entitled, "An act to establish a territorial government for Utah," providing for the organization of Utah Territory, which was signed by President Millard Fillmore, and went into force on the 9th of September, 1850. The President appointed officers for the Territory as follows: Brigham Young, Governor; B. D. Harris, Secretary; Joseph Buffington, Chief Justice; Perry C. Brocchus and Zerubbabel Snow, Associate Justices; Seth M. Blair, Attorney; and Joseph L. Heywood, Marshal.

The news of the organization of the Territory and the appointment of the Governor and other officers did not reach the valley until January 27th, 1851, being even then unofficially conveyed by way of San Francisco, through New York newspapers which were brought to Salt Lake by Mr. Henry E. Gibson.

On the 5th of April, 1851, Governor Young, who had taken the oath of office on the 3rd of February, dissolved the General Assembly of the State of Deseret, and thus changed the provisional to the territorial form of government, merging the State into the Territory of Utah.

Among the more important of the many acts of the Provisional Assembly, afterward made legal by the territorial legislature, may be mentioned the creation of Salt Lake, Weber, Utah, Sanpete, Juab and Tooele counties, and the granting of a charter to the University of Deseret, in the winter of 1849-50; the passing of acts incorporating Great Salt Lake City (January 9th), Ogden City, the city of Manti, Provo City and Parowan City (February 6th), and the Church of Jesus Christ of Latter-day Saints (February 8th), in 1851.

On the first Monday of August, 1851, an election was held, at which were chosen a Delegate to Congress, Dr. Bernhisel, who was the first to represent Utah in that body, and a legislature.

With the arrival of Judge Brocchus, in August, all the federal judges were in the territory, and had been assigned by the Governor to their districts. Judge Brocchus (who was appointed with Secretary Harris and Judge Brandebury instead of Mr. Buffington, declined), soon became dissatisfied with his position, being doubtless disappointed in not being elected by the Mormons to Congress. The result of this disaffection was a breach, which was a beginning of the long controversy between the federal judges and the Mormons.

Being invited to speak at a public meeting early in September, Judge Brocchus shamefully abused the people and their institutions. He was severely rebuked by President Young. Not long after this episode, the Secretary and the two Judges informed the Governor that they would return to Washington. They did so on September 28th, carrying with them the Territorial seal, records and documents, as well as $24,000.00 appropriated by Congress for the *per diem* of the legislature. These "runaway judges and secretary," by which sobriquet they became known, made their report to the proper national officials, falsely asserting that they were forced to leave Utah on account of the lawless acts and seditious tendencies of

Governor Brigham Young and the majority of the citizens. Their scheme to create trouble for the Mormons did not succeed, however, as they had expected, for they were forced to retire, the President appointing in their stead, on the 15th of August, 1852, Lazarus H. Reed, chief justice, with Leonidas Shaver, associate, and Benjamin G. Ferris, of anti-Mormon book fame, secretary. The vacancies in the meantime were temporarily filled by gubernatorial appointment, a full explanation being rendered to the President of the United States. The next federal officials were Chief Justice John F. Kinney, appointed August 24th, 1854, Associate Justice George P. Stiles, August 1st, 1854; Judge W. W. Drummond, September 12th, 1854. The latter two became chiefly instrumental in bringing about the "Utah War."

While these political changes were being made, other more important events were transpiring among the people of Utah. Desiring a closer association with the other citizens of the Union, the Governor and legislative Assembly as early as March 3rd, 1852, memorialized Congress for the construction of a national central railroad to the Pacific coast, also for a telegraph line, setting forth among other things as their reasons for this desire "that the immense emigration to and from the Pacific requires the immediate attention, guardian care and fostering assistance of the greatest and most liberal government on the face of the earth." "That an eligible route can be obtained—that the mineral resources of California and these mountains can never be fully developed to the benefit of the people of the United States without the construction of such a road; and upon its completion the entire trade of China and the East Indies will pass through the heart of the Union, thereby giving our citizens almost the control of the Asiatic and Pacific trade, pouring into the lap of the American states the millions that are now diverted through other commercial channels." Again, in Governor Young's message to the legislature, in 1853, he urges the necessity of a national iron highway, and calls attention to the importance of properly presenting the matter. before Congress. A great mass meeting was accordingly held in January, 1854, in which the people took steps to further memorialize Congress for the construction of a railway via Salt Lake City to the Pacific. But other petitions were necessary, and over fifteen years were to elapse before the iron horse should awake the echoes in their mountain retreat.

With the arrival of fresh emigrants, the growth and extension of the cities and villages continued, until there was a chain of thirty Mormon settlements from Bear River, on the north, to the rim of the Great Basin, on the south, and to the east and west of Salt Lake City. Public buildings and stores were erected, coal and iron mines developed, grist and saw mills were busy in all parts. Encouraged by legislative appropriation and protection, home manufacturing establishments sprang up in various places. Ten thousand dollars of the territorial revenue of something over twenty-six thousand, were expended for fostering infant industries, for surveys, roads and bridges, and for educational purposes. It should be remembered that among the Mormons colonizers, the school house was the first public building to be erected in every settlement.

On April 6th, 1853, the corner stone of the now completed great temple at Salt Lake City was laid, ground having been broken for the foundation on the 14th of February previous. It was dedicated forty years later, April 6th, 1893, and has been pronounced " a structure unsurpassed if not unequaled for beauty and sublimity by any other edifice in America."

At the October Conference, 1853, many were called to strengthen the settlements in Iron, Tooele, Sanpete, Box Elder and Juab counties.

As a rule only little trouble was experienced with the Indians, owing chiefly to the wise course adopted by President Young in treating them. His life-long policy toward the red men, which has saved much property and many lives in Utah, is embodied in this utterance of his which he ever put faithfully into practice as a private individual, as Governor and Government Indian Agent, and as President of the Church: "It is cheaper to feed the Indians than to fight them." But their treatment under these conditions, and with the careful diplomacy of the great Mormon leader did not entirely prevent conflicts with them. The first troubles occurred in 1850-1. Then followed a period of peace until 1853, when the Ute war broke out, instigated doubtless by Mexican traders, who came to Utah and supplied the Indians with firearms, ammunition, horses, etc., taking in exchange Indian women and children, who were subsequently sold into slavery. Governor Young proclaimed against this traffic, which displeased both traders and Indians. Passing emigrants also did much injury by shooting Indians without cause. In the spring of 1854, the trouble was ended in a treaty of peace. As a result of the conflict, about twenty whites and a large number of Indians were killed, while the people and the Territory together suffered a loss of about $300,000.00.

The chief item of religious interest was the public avowal of polygamy, at a conference of the Church in

Salt Lake City, August 29th, 1852. Plural marriage, included in the doctrine of celestial marriage, was practiced long before this time by the Saints in Nauvoo, Winter Quarters, and also in Utah. It was first made known to Joseph Smith, the Prophet, in 1831, and in Nauvoo, in 1841, was introduced by him to a number of leading Elders, and practiced by them and the Prophet. The revelation on celestial marriage was recorded July 12th, 1843. Celestial marriage may, but does not necessarily, include a plurality of wives; it consists of the eternity of the marriage covenant between man and wife. When a marriage is sealed by the Holy Priesthood, which has power to bind on earth and it is bound in heaven, the man and wife have not alone claim upon each other in time, but in eternity also—they are husband and wife after the resurrection. The doctrine revolutionizes the idea of marriage as entertained by mankind in general, which is usually considered to be a contract lasting only in this life; and declares that the association of the sexes thus entered into is eternal, that our relations here as husbands, wives, families, continue in the celestial spheres. Marriage thus becomes one of the chief means of man's exaltation and glory in the world to come, whereby he may have endless increase of eternal lives, and attain at length to the power of the Godhead. It was this glorious doctrine, in connection with baptism, redemption and sealing for the dead, that was the uppermost theme of the Prophet Joseph during the last two years or more of his life.

On this August day here amidst the liberty of the mountains, Brigham Young saw fit to publicly proclaim this consoling doctrine including also that portion of it relating to a plurality of wives—the latter a principle which Joseph and the leading Elders only had heretofore privately entertained and practiced because it came in conflict with the prejudice, education, traditions and sentiments of the age. Then followed the promulgation of the doctrine by missionaries to the whole world. Afterward polygamy became the leading question for contention between the officers of the Government and the Mormons, until the practice was finally suspended by a manifesto of President Wilford Woodruff, dated September 24th, 1890. At the following October Conference the Church accepted his declaration as authoritative and binding, and a plurality of wives is now neither taught nor practiced. But marriages for time and eternity are entered into by all the faithful Saints in the holy temples which dot the landscape of their Zion.

EVENTS FROM 1854 TO 1857.

As Governor Young's first term was drawing to a close, it became evident that the false stories circulated about him and his people, chiefly by the "runaways" and by Secretary Ferris, had so influenced the Nation's Executive that he would not appoint the Mormon Governor for a second term. The action of Colonel E. J. Steptoe, however, changed his determination. The Colonel arrived in Utah in August, 1854, with a detachment of troops on his way to California. To him President Franklin Pierce tendered the governorship. This the Colonel respectfully declined, and, with leading citizens, Mormon and non-Mormon, federal officials and army officers, petitioned for the re-appointment of the present incumbent. The memorial had the desired effect. The request was granted, and Brigham Young received the appointment as Governor and Superintendent of Indian Affairs.

Colonel Steptoe remained with his troops in the territory over winter, continuing on good terms with the Mormons. He had orders to arrest and bring to trial the perpetrators of the Gunnison massacre,* which he succeeded in doing. Eight Indians being arrested were tried for murder; among them was the chief Kanosh, who, with four others, was acquitted, while a verdict of manslaughter was returned against the remaining three.

In the spring of 1855 Morgan County was settled by Jedediah Morgan Grant. Orson Hyde pushed west and established a colony in Carson Valley, now in Nevada. During the Buchanan War the settlements in that valley were broken up.

On the 10th of May, 1855, Charles C. Rich, George Q. Cannon, Joseph Bull and others left for San Francisco. There Elder Cannon established the weekly *Westen Standard*, publishing the first issue on the 23rd of February, 1856, about which time his translation of the Book of Mormon in the Hawaiian language also appeared.

Judge George P. Stiles succeeded Judge Snow at the expiration of the latter's term in 1854. After the death of Chief Justice Reed, in New York in March, 1855, Judge John F. Kinney was appointed to succeed him. Judge Leonidas Shaver died in Salt Lake City, June 29th, 1855, and was succeeded by Judge W. W.

---

*Lieutenant John W. Gunnison, afterward Captain, had assisted Captain Stansbury in his labors. Encamped on the Sevier engaged in surveying a railway route, he was cruelly killed by the Indians. October 25th, 1853. Gunnison, Sanpete County, was named in honor of this friend of Utah and her people. He wrote a valuable and impartial work on "The Mormons."

Drummond. Both Judges Reed and Shaver were greatly respected by the people, who sincerely mourned their death.

The Legislature met for the first time in Fillmore, the new capital of the territory, on the 10th of December, 1855. In January of the following year the populaion of the territory is given as 76,335. During this session another unsuccessful effort was made for the admission of Utah into the Union. John Taylor, then editor of the *Mormon*, in New York, and George A. Smith, were elected delegates to present the memorial and constitution to Congress. Cache and Box Elder Counties were created, besides a number of counties in Carson Valley.

The crops of 1854-5 had failed owing to drought and grasshoppers. The winter of 1855-6 was unusually severe. Cattle and sheep by the thousands died from cold and starvation. As a result of these combined calamities the Saints suffered greatly and were once more driven to roots for subsistence. Some there were who had provided for the famine, but their little stores were soon exhausted by their willingness to help the needy. Those who had gave to those who had not. Much suffering was thus relieved or prevented. "Unity and equality—those watchwords of the United Order—were once more emphasized in the dealings of the Mormon people with one another and with the needy of all classes and creeds among them."*

To add to the troubles of these times, the Indians precipitated another war known as the Tintic War. It

---

* Whitney's Utah, Vol. 1, p. 548.

caused the death of twelve of the settlers. Indian depredations on the plains were also numerous in 1856.

But that year's greatest calamity, penetrating the whole Church with its grief and gloom, befel the late handcart companies. "It had been decided by the Mormon leaders that a cheaper and more expeditious method of bringing the emigrants across the great plains would be by handcarts in lieu of ox-teams and wagons. The carts, manufactured on the frontier, were to carry the baggage and provisions, and the stronger men were to pull them."* There were in all five companies of emigrating Saints. mostly from England, who had decided to cross the plains in that way, traversing deserts, wading rivers, climbing mountains, a distance of thirteen hundred miles to Salt Lake City. Three companies arrived in the Valley after a three months' journey, comparatively in good condition; but the last two were caught in the snows and the storms of an early winter. After suffering starvation and untold hardships, their remnants finally arrived in the Valley, the last delayed company, composed of six hundred persons, having lost more than one-fourth of their numbers by death. All would have shared the same fate had not relief parties, risking their own lives, gone to their assistance.

---

10. THE UTAH EXPEDITION.

While Judges Reed and Shaver had been regarded with much favor by the Mormons, and Judge Kinney was now so regarded, it was evident from the first that

---

* For full accounts of the hand cart companies, written by John Chislett and John Jaques, see Whitney's Utah, Vol. 1, pp. 558-564.

Judges Stiles and Drummond would not so be considered. The reason is plain. Their characters were so low and vicious as to command no respect. The former was a characterless renegade Mormon, the latter a gambler and a lecher.* And these two men, but more especially Drummond, did more than any others to bring about the trouble wich is known as the "Mormon War," or properly speaking, President "Buchanan's egregious blunder."

Little attention had been paid by the general government to Utah. It had taken occasion to slight her and her just demands in the matters of admission to the sisterhood of states, and in appropriations such as were made to other territories for the expense of their legislatures, state houses, Indian outbreaks, etc. Then to make matters worse, such political adventurers as have been named were sent to be the judges of the people. These, finding no sympathy among an honest community, laid plans to still aggravate the existing suspicions and indifference of the nation toward the Mormons.

Finding their courts overcrowded after the departure of the "runaway judges," the Utah Legislature passed an act in 1852 giving the probate courts "power to exercise original jurisdiction, both civil and criminal, as well in chancery as in common law, when not prohibited by legislative enactment." Thus arose complications. The federal judges declared that these courts nullified the powers of the higher tribunals, while the Mormons maintained that without the powers of the probate

---

*Speaking of Drummond, Bancroft, History of Utah, p. 490, says: "Leaving his wife and family in Illinois without the means of support, he brought with him a harlot whom he had picked up in the streets of Washington, and introducing her as Mrs. Drummond, seated her by his side on the judicial bench."

courts they would be left practically without civil and criminal jurisdiction. Judges Stiles and Drummond, contrary to the practice of their predecessors, made a direct issue by ignoring the authority of the lower courts and their officials. The people would not sustain them in this movement, and being powerless to proceed, Judge Stiles was compelled to adjourn his court. Returning to Washington in the spring of 1857, he made affidavit to this effect, declaring among other things that his records had been burnt and he threatened with violence. The records, it is true, had been removed from his office, but were in safe-keeping, being later produced. But his report went abroad creating much adverse criticism of the Mormons.

Judge Drummond became very unpopular not alone for moral reasons, but also for his judicial course. At length he concluded to resign. His letter of resignation, dated March 30th, 1857, sent to Attorney-General Jeremiah S. Black, sets forth his reasons for this action. He conjures up many wicked lies and groundless accusations. He charges that the records, papers, etc., of the supreme court have been destroyed by order of the Church; that the federal officers are constantly insulted, harassed and annoyed, without redress. He charges the Governor with improperly pardoning criminals, advising jurors beforehand, so that no charges but his are obeyed. The judiciary is treated as a farce, the "officers are insulted, harassed and murdered for doing their duty." Closing, he suggests that a new Governor be appointed and "supported with a sufficient military aid."

This report and a letter written by a mail contractor named W. F. Magraw, also minor complaints from Indian agents and federal officials, led President Buchanan without further investigation to conclude that a rebellion existed in Utah. It has also been said that he was instigated by a rebellious desire to scatter the Union forces in case of a conflict with the South on the slavery question, which was then the uppermost topic in the country. The Mormons, then as now and ever, loyal to their country and its institutions, made answer to all the charges as they were published, but their explanations were deemed insufficient. Brigham Young was superseded in the governorship by Alfred Cumming, and an army of two thousand five hundred men, well equipped and supplied, was organized and ordered to march to Salt Lake City, ostensibly as a *posse comitatus* to sustain his authority, or if need be to put down the alleged lawlessness by force. The commander of the troops was instructed under date of June 29th, 1857 how to proceed.

The mails to Utah had been stopped, leaving the Mormons as ignorant of the coming of the army as they were of having rebelled against their country. It was not until the 24th of July, while patriotically celebrating their advent into the territory ten years before, that President Young and his people were apprised of the startling news by three Mormon messengers from the east. In the evening President Young called the people together, and addressing them said among other expressions: "Liars have reported that this people have committed treason, and upon their misrepresentations the President has ordered out troops to assist in officering this territory. * * * We have transgressed no law, neither do we intend to do so; but as for any nation coming to destroy this people, God Almighty being my helper it shall not be." Then the celebration went on. There was no excitement, but war became the uppermost theme thereafter.

On the 8th of September Captain Van Vliet arrived in Salt Lake City, meeting with a cordial reception; his mission was to purchase supplies and to inform the Mormons that the government would not molest or interfere with them. The object of sending the troops was to install the new officials.

"I believe you tell the truth," replied Brigham, in an interview on Septembr 9th, "that you believe this,—but you do not know their intentions as well as I do. * * * We have plenty here of what you want, but we will sell you nothing. Further than this, your army shall not enter this valley."

President Young's experience with military bodies in Missouri and Illinois, had led him to lose confidence in their asserted designs, and to be suspicious of their intents. Why had not the officers been sent without the army? There had been no resistance to the civil authorities heretofore, why was it now necessary to install them by the aid of troops? The real design was evidently hidden. It was the extermination of the Mormons, the spoilation of their homes and possessions, their complete annihilation. So thought Brigham Young, and he dealt accordingly.

The Captain remonstrated saying that even if the mountain passes could be defended against the army now coming, reinforcements would be sent the following season to overcome all opposition. To which President Young replied: "We are aware that such will be the case; but when these troops arrive they will find Utah a desert; every house will be burned to the ground, every tree cut down, and every field laid waste."

The Captain was as deeply impressed as he was astonished. He returned to Washington to report to the Secretary of War.

Following the Captain's departure, Governor Young declared the territory under martial law, September 17th. The Nauvoo Legion was thoroughly organized under Lieutenant Daniel H. Wells, and two thousand five hundred men, young and old, were mustered to prevent the entrance of the troops into the Valley. Early in October the government army supply trains were burned at Green River by Lot Smith, followed by the destruction of Fort Bridger. Finally the invading troops, crippled, starved and frozen, were forced to go into winter quarters on Black's Fork. Excepting a guard, the Utah militia returned to their homes early in December. So matters rested until spring, when it was fully expected the conflict would begin anew.

Meanwhile Governor Young had asked Colonel Kane to present the true situation before President Buchanan. Having done so, the President dispatched the Colonel to Utah as private Government envoy with a conciliatory message. He reached Salt Lake City February 25th, 1858, and learned that there would be no objections to the entrance of the new governor without the army, which would not be allowed to accompany him or to quarter in any city or settlement of the territory. Departing over the snows for Black's Fork Colonel Kane soon convinced Governor Cumming that he had no need of the army. Then the two departed for Salt Lake City, arriving there, April 12th. After a cordial meeting with President Young, Governor Cumming was duly and peaceably installed in his new position. His noble peace mission now ended, Colonel Kane returned to report his success in Washington.

What was now to be done with the army?

In June, Governor Powell of Kentucky, and Major McKulloch of Texas, met President Young as a Peace Commission in Salt Lake City, bearing from the national Executive a full and free pardon for all past seditions and treasons for all of the Mormons who would submit to national authority.

President Young stated his position: "I thank President Buchanan for forgiving me, but I really cannot tell what I have done. I know one thing, and that is, that the people called Mormons are a loyal and law-abiding people, and have ever been. It is true Lot Smith burned some wagons containing government supplies for the army. This was an overt act, and if it is for this that we are to be pardoned, I accept the pardon."

It was then agreed that the army might come into the basin, but should not quarter within forty miles of the city, nor in any settlement of the territory. Entering Salt Lake City June 26th, they founded Camp Floyd, thirty-six miles south, where they remained until 1860. The last remnant departed in 1861. Many of the soldiers participated in the Civil War, in which Albert Sidney Johnston, the commander of the Buchanan Expedition against the Mormons, took part as a rebel.

Upon first entering the Valley, the troops were deeply moved by the desolation which they witnessed all about them. With no faith in the promises of armies, the Saints, thirty thousand strong, had fled south to what destination they knew not. Their deserted villages and cities were inhabited only by the guards who had been left with torch in hand ready to fire their dearly-earned homes and possessions, in case the hostile army should invade their land to repeat the scenes of Far West and Nauvoo. In vain Governor Cumming pleaded with them to remain. Said President Young: "We know all about it, Governor. We have on just such occasions seen our disarmed men hewn down in cold blood, our virgin daughters violated, our wives ravished to death before our eyes. We know all about it, Governor Cumming."

"The Move" attracted the attention to the sacrifice of this people and the wrongs inflicted upon them, redounding to their praise in the press of Europe and the Union. The public saw in it heroism, devotion, sincerity. The tide turned in favor of the Mormons. When the object of "the move" had thus been realized, the people returned to their cities and habitations which had been placed sincerely upon the altar of sacrifice, but this time not required of them.

Thus ended the "war." It had cost the country fifteen million dollars, exposed the government to ridicule, and accomplished nothing; but it won for the Mormons esteem, respect, a recognition by the outside world of their devotion to principle, their bravery in time of peril, their loyalty to country.

11. A PERIOD OF RECUPERATION.

The time between the departure of the army and the advent of the great trans-continental railway line may aptly be termed a recuperation period in the history of the Saints. During these years they not only advanced in spiritual things possibly to a greater degree than heretofore since their arrival in the valleys of the mountains, but they prospered more abundantly in temporal affairs. It was an epoch of telegraphs, railways, and trade.

Owing in a degree to the vicissitudes of 1854-5-6, many of the members of the Church had become weary in their incessant struggle with harships. This condition led to neglect of duty, which in turn resulted in the loss of faith, accompanied by moral transgression. Every triumph that the Saints had so for achieved in their wonderful career, had been won by and through their faith. Religion had been their stimulant, their support. So it must continue. To this end the "reformation" was begun, to revive the lost faith of the indifferent and sinful. Its labors began at a conference at Kaysville, September 15th, 1856, spreading thence throughout the entire Church, at home and abroad, continuing with much enthusiasm into the spring and summer of 1857. Bishops, missionaries and leading Elders everywhere took part. Repentance, a turning way from pride, covetousness, physical and moral uncleanliness, and other abominations, were required of the people. Humility prevailed, and there was a general renewal of covenants, so that the Saints again found favor in the sight of God. Thus this movement, while perhaps overdone in some instances, resulted as a whole in much good. Without the resulting purification, it is doubtful whether there would have been so general a response to the sacrifices of "The Move," or such a healthy growth in the years following.

The Overland Telegraph was completed October 24th, 1861. Less than three years and three months had passed since the memorable day in the world's history, August 5th, 1858, when the first Atlantic cable was completed. Now the electric messenger penetrated the continent and bore its instant tales from sea to sea, through the home of the Saints, placing them in immediate communication with the whole world. It was the signal of a new era about to dawn upon them, but they were preparing themselves for the changes that it would bring. The facility with which the Mormons adapt themselves to progressive, altered conditions, has often been a subject of remark. The present case was no exception.

Torn as the nation was at this time by internal strife, it is a significant commentary upon Mormon loyalty that the first message which passed east over the completed line from President Brigham Young read: "Utah has not seceded, but is firm for the Constitution and laws of our once happy country."

In 1862 another unsuccessful trial was made by the Saints to obtain statehood for Utah. Hons. William H. Hooper and George Q. Cannon were the senators-elect. They labored diligently to secure Utah's admission to the sisterhood of states, their motto being: "We can redress our grievances better in the Union than out of it," significant words, indeed, in view of the great national controversy over secession. It was on the 2nd day of July of this same year that President Abraham Lincoln approved and signed "an act to punish and prevent the practice of polygamy in the territories of the United States and other places, and disapproving and annulling certain acts of the Legislative Assembly of the Territory of Utah." The provisions of this act became a dead-letter upon the statute-books for many years. There was, however, an effort made by Governor Harding, in 1863, to punish President Young under this law, but for lack of evidence the jury failed to indict, and so the matter rested. It being President Lincoln's policy to let the Mormons alone, Governor Harding upon their petition was dismissed for his pains. Then followed a time of political peace, broken only by the efforts of Col. P. E. Connor to establish a military in lieu of a civil government in the territory. Col. Connor is credited with being "the father of Utah mining," he was the founder of Camp or Fort Douglas, and his troops, California volunteers who had enlisted seven hundred strong to fight Southern rebels, being detained in Utah did good service in checking Indian depredations north of Cache Valley, for which the Col. was made Brigadier-General. But his scheme to establish military power in Utah utterly failed.

The next important event was the establishment of the Deseret Telegraph line. With little ready means, the Mormons built five hundred miles of this line, between 1865 and 1867, at a cost of $150.00 per mile, thus placing their principal settlements, now extending in all directions, into instant communication with each other and with the leaders of the Church, whose counsels and instructions thus could be transmitted rapidly to every portion of the territory.

In 1868, the approaching railroad warned the inspired leader of the Saints that the isolation which had made Zion a peculiar people would soon be destroyed. There would be great financial and social changes. To guard the money interests of the people, as well as to insure their temporal supremacy, President Young announced, "that it was advisable that the people of Utah should become their own merchants." Then followed the organization of Zion's Co-operative Mercantile Institution, which began business early in 1869. Branches were established in nearly all the settlements, and while many have gone out of business, there can be no question about the benefit that resulted to the community from this movement. There are several branches of the institution today. The parent house has an enormous trade, and may be said to constitute the temporal bulwark of the Mormons. It has helped materially to preserve them as a communty; it has earned for them a financial influence abroad, while it has maintained a uniformity in prices, and has been a ballast to trade at home; it has held the money resources of the people within themselves, and in great measure it has insured the social unity of the Saints.

The Union Pacific Railway was completed as far as Salt Lake Valley on the 8th of March, 1869. At length the petitions and desires of the Utah pioneers were answered. But their influence was not all that was offered to aid in this monstrous enterprise. With their own hands, the Mormons graded the highway from the head of Echo Canyon to Ogden City. Its eastern end traverses the plains for many hundred miles over the road which they pioneered. At Ogden City, the eventful day named, the assembled multitude now greeted the iron horse with shouts of, "Utah bids you welcome;" "Hail to the great national highway." On the 17th of May following, the Utah Central Railroad, from Ogden to Salt Lake City, was begun, being completed on the 10th of January, 1870. It was purely a Mormon enterprise. Then followed the building of the Utah Southern (May 1871), and the Utah and Northern (September 1871).

In the meantime missionaries were constantly sent to the nations of the earth, and emigrations, for which hundreds of teams yearly were forwarded to the Missouri, from various lands continued to swell the population.

New settlements were formed.* Thrift and industry made the barren places fruitful.† The thirsty plains and and valleys smiled with verdure at the touch of the magic streams directed by the toiling husbandman. Peace prevailed in the mountain Zion.‡ Children listened with wonder to the tale of the pioneer. Schools and meeting houses§ sprang up in every village, atteded by a happy youth and a thankful people, content in their homespun. Virtue dwelt by the side of honesty, and the fear of God, in the hearts of the people.

OFFICIAL CRUSADE—DEATH OF PRESIDENT YOUNG.

With the introduction of President Young's mercantile policy arose a schism, known as the "Godbeite" or "New Movement," which threatened a dangerous break in the Church. A number of disaffected Mormon merchants began to oppose President Young, and what they termed his "one man power," his temporal leanings, exemplified in the organization of Z. C. M. I., the build-

---

* Bear Lake Valley and Wasatch County were settled in 1863; Sevier and Piute Counties, in 1864.

† Portions of the Territory were severely afflicted by the grasshoppers which pest appeared in 1867 and continued until well along into the 70's, often totally destroying vegetation for years together.

‡ The exception to this was the Black Hawk Indian trouble in 1866-7, in southern counties The Utah militia, under Gen. D. H. Wells, did good service in protecting the settlements.

§ The tabernacle at Salt Lake City was so far completed in 1867 that the October conference was held therein. At this time Joseph F. Smith was called and ordained to the Apostleship.

The "*Deseret News*" was first issued as a daily in Nov., 1867; as a weekly. June 15th, 1850; as a semi weekly, October 8th, 1865. The Ogden *Junction* was first issued January 1st, 1870, and the Salt Lake Daily *Herald*, June 6th. 1870.

ing of railroads and other secular enterprises. These Elders, being excommunicated and joined by anti-Mormons, became the nucleus of home opposition from which grew, in the early months of 1870, the so called Liberal Party whose bitter and unscrupulous warfare against the Saints is almost without a parallel in the history of political strife. To the agitations and misrepresentations of this party, coupled with the co-operation of Mr. Schyler Colfax, Reverend J. P. Newman, and conspirators and allies at the seat of Government, may be attributed the missionary judicial crusade that overwhelmed the Church and its leading men with persecution, under the administration of President U. S. Grant, in 1870-1 to 1875. While Mr. Colfax and his eastern associates were doubtless sincere in their desire to fight polygamy, the overthrow of which was the aim of their warfare, no one doubts that their allies in Utah had solely another object in view—the political control of the Territory—they were determined to rule or ruin.

President Grant was inaugurated on March 4th, 1869. The "let them alone" policy of President Lincoln was from now on abandoned by the President who, thoroughly filled with the misrepresentations of the party and their allies referred to, determined to solve the Mormon problem, termed the "twin relic," by special legislation and judicial machinery, or, these failing, by the sword as slavery had been determined. It is claimed by the "new movement" people that they averted a war, in other words induced the administration to abandon to some extent a proposed military subjugation of the Terirtory. It was now decided to proceed against the Mormons through appointed federal officials. To begin with the proper men were found in Governor J. Wilson Shaffer and Chief Justice James B. McKean, the most determined foes that Utah ever had. To aid them in their bigoted mission, the Government sent soldiers to act as a "moral force" in the protection of Gentiles and apostates. Small wonder that illegal processes, packed juries, absurd rulings characterized the judicial proceedings. Where the law failed to aid them in carrying out their measures, they did not scruple to set it aside by extra-judicial rulings.

The muster of the Territorial militia was first forbidden by Governor Shaffer in 1870, evidently that greater scope might be given the officers to harass the Saints without danger of resistance. The militia had often been called into action to protect the settlements from Indian depredations, serving weeks at a time without pay either from the Territory or the general Government. But from this time on, they were not even allowed to patriotically parade in a 4th of July procession, or upon any other public occasion. In October, 1870, Governor Shaffer died and was succeeded by Governor George L. Woods who followed in his footsteps.

The militia was practically disbanded, followed by high-handed judicial acts of Judge McKean, who disgraced his office "in a manner to which the world can furnish no parallel." His mission was to overthrow Mormonism. "A mission," he declared, "as high above my mere duty as judge as heaven is above the earth." Raising the cry: Federal authority vs. polygamic theocracy, the crusade was carried on in deadly earnest until, his illegal decisions were reversed by the Supreme Court of the United States. President Young and other prominent men of the Church suffered severe annoyances through arrests and through illegally instituted judicial proceedings, being forced to incur great expense in defending themselves. At length Judge McKean went to such extremes that the administration, in sympathy with him as it was, could tolerate his actions no longer, and on the 16th of March, 1875, he was removed because of his fanatical and extreme conduct, and because of several acts of his which the President considered ill advised, tyrannical, and in excess of his powers as Judge. But the Liberals continued their machinations unabated. Nearly every session of Congress was overwhelmed by bills of their framing and concoction, calculated to proscribe or persecute the Saints. The "Poland Bill" was passed June 23rd, 1874. Their agitations finally resulted in the passage of the "Edmunds' Bill," in 1882, supplemented later by the "Edmunds-Tucker Act."

In the midst of these persecutions and annoyances, the interests of the Church never lagged for a moment. Colonization also continued. An effort was made in 1873 to establish settlements in Arizona. A large number of settlers from Utah met in Salt Lake City, March 8th, and were instructed in their colonizing labors by President Young. Meeting at first with failure, their efforts resulted in the experience which finally led to success, and at present there are many thriving settlements of the Saints in Arizona.

On the 14th of October, the year previous, President George A. Smith left on a trip to Palestine, where, on March 2nd following, he and his associates held divine service on the Mount of Olives, on which occasion they dedicated the Land of Palestine for the gathering of the Jews, and for the re-building of Jerusalem.* Returning,

* "When you get to the land of Palestine, we want you to dedicate and consecrate that land to the Lord, that it may be blessed with fruitfulness, pre-

President Smith reached Salt Lake City, June 18th, 1873, where he died, September 1st, 1875.

In 1874-5 there was a general religious movement among the Indians, hundreds embracing the gospel in Tooele County, St. George, and other places. In January of the latter year the first Lamanites were married according to the order of the Holy Priesthood.

In the summer of 1875, the Improvement Associations of the young Latter-day Saints were first organized. Four years later, their organ, the *Contributor*, first appeared (October, 1879.) The membership of these associations now numbers tens of thousands of the sons and daughters of the Mormons. The Sunday Schools, first organized in the Fourteenth Ward, Salt Lake City, by Elder Richard Ballantyne, in 1849, had flourished and increased in membership to nearly thirty thousand.[*] Secular education was not neglected. Every settlement boasted its schoolhouse and public school which compared favorably with like institutions in the States or Territories of equal age, in other parts of the Union. President Young established the B. Y. Academy at Provo, October 16th, 1875, and the B. Y. College in Logan, July 24th, 1877. The Deseret University opened for the first time November 11th, 1850, was prospering. The leaders of the Church have ever been firm friends of true education, and their efforts in this direction have ever been nobly seconded by the Saints as a community;

---

paratory to the return of the Jews, in fulfillment of prophecy and the accomplishment of the purposes of our Heavenly Father"—Excerpt from a letter by Presidents Brigham Young and Daniel H. Wells to President Smith.

[*] The *Juvenile Instructor*, established January 1st, 1866, is the organ of the Sabbath Schools of the Saints.

as a result, Utah stands today first in educational progress among her sister commonwealths in the west.*

Temple building went on. The St. George Temple was dedicated at the April conference held in that city, April 6-8, 1877, ordinances for the dead being ministered therein on the 9th. On the 25th of this same month, the temple site in Manti was dedicated, followed, May 18th, by the dedication of the ground for the Logan temple.

The organization of the Stakes of Zion was completed in the summer of 1877, the quorums of the Priesthood were set in order, and the ecclesiastical government was perfected according to the pattern revealed from heaven. In this pleasant labor the Founder of Utah spent his last days.

On the 29th day of August, 1877, President Brigham Young died, surrounded by his family and kind friends. He passed peacefully to rest sincerely mourned by a whole people whose chief and adviser he had been for thirty three years. He was one of the great men of the century. His achievements as leader of the Nauvoo Exodus, and as Colonizer of the American desert, will be regarded as among the grandest accomplishments of modern times.

---

*The *School Journal*, reviewing the school exhibits of the various states and territories at the world's Exposition (1893), says: "In the originality an t general merit of its exhibit, Utah stands easily first in the Western group. * * Here behind the western mountains a system of education is being matured, that, while it challenges the best elsewhere, owes its upbuilding very greatly to the peculiar stamina of its own communities."

FROM THE DEATH OF PRESIDENT YOUNG TO THE PRESENT TIME.
1877-1893.

1. John Taylor Chosen Leader.

Enemies of theSaints had often prophesied that upon the death of Brigham Young Mormonism would fall to pieces. It was soon clearly demonstrated, however, that the Church is not founded upon the ability or strength of any man, but rather upon revelation, with Christ as its corner stone.

The order of succession had been decided in Nauvoo. Apostle John Taylor, who was president of the Twelve, with his quorum now became the presiding authority of the Church. As such they were unanimously upheld at the 48th semi-annual conference, in October, 1877. On this occasion the authorities of the Church were sustained in their order; first, by the Priesthood of the Church who voted by quorums, from the highest in authority to the lowest, rising in turns to their feet with uplifted hands; then, finally, by the entire congregation. There was a spirit of union which so far from boding dissolution, rather indicated renewed strength, unfaltering devotion to their cause and doctrine.

At the October conference, 1880, three years afterward, the First Presidency was organized for the third time in the history of the Church. John Taylor was chosen President, with George Q. Cannon and Joseph F. Smith as his counselors. President Taylor was then 72 years of age. He was a native of Milnthorp, England, born November 1st, 1808. He joined the Church in Canada in 1836, and was called to the Apostleship by revelation, in 1838. He had filled numerous missions to England, France (into which land he introduced the gospel), Germany and the United States. He had extensively engaged in literary labors, having edited Church papers in every country named save England, besides superintending the translation of the Book of Mormon into French and German, supplemented at that time and later by the publication of important doctrinal works. He was a dear friend of the Prophet Joseph, they having mingled blood at the martyrdom. In all the travels of the Saints, and in their mountain home, he had always been a leader in their midst. The people had full confidence in him; he was their "Champion of Liberty." Fifty years had passed since six members met in the State of New York and organized the Church of Jesus Christ of Latter-day Saints. Like the ancient, modern Israel would have a year of jubilee. That the people might feel its influence, it was agreed at the regular April conference, 1880, on suggestion of President Taylor, to release one half of the people's indebtedness to the Perpetual Emigrating Fund, the principal of which amounted to $704,000, and now, with interest added, to $1,604,000. Out of this amount it was voted to forgive the poo debtors $800,000, or about one-half of the whole amount, the other half being left for such debtors to pay as were able but had not done so. Then there was due the Church on tithing account $151,798, $75,899 of which were canceled on the indebtedness of the deserving poor. It was also agreed to distribute to the worthy poor one-thousand good cows, the Church to furnish 300, and the stakes, 700; also 5000 sheep, 2000 of which were donated by the Church and the remainder by the stakes.

The year 1879 had been very dry causing a shortage in crops. There was little wheat in the Territory, and so the sisters of the Relief Societies voted to loan out to the needy farmers 34,761 bushels of seed wheat, to be returned at their convenience without interest.

It was to. be made a year of rejoicing. Individuals were counseled to relieve their distressed debtors; Z. C. M. I. and the banks were asked to do something in cancelling the debts of the honest poor. The utmost good feeling prevailed, and the Saints generally carried out the counsel of their leader: "While God is blessing us, let us bless one another."

Pioneer day was celebrated this year with great rejoicings and demonstrations in Salt Lake City, people coming from all parts of the Territory on the occasion. The trades, industries, schools, societies and associations,* commerce, art and sciences, were duly represented in the great parade. After the grand procession, appropriate reminiscent ceremonies were held in the large Tabernacle. Among the noteworthy parts of the progarm was the appearance of twenty-five representatives from as many nations where the gospel had been preached.

In the concluding speech on this occasion, President Taylor made this remarkable prophetic utterance: "There are events in the future, and not very far ahead, that will require all our faith, all our energy, all our confidence, all our trust in God to enable us to withstand the influences that will be brought against us. * * *

---

*The Sabbath schools at this time numbered 33,000; the Improvement Associations of the young men were ten thousand strong.

There never was a time when we needed to be more humble and more prayerful; there never was a time when we needed more fidelity, self-denial and adherence to the principles of truth, than we do this day."

So indeed it proved to be. The next few years were to be among the most trying in the experience of the Church.

2. THE EDMUNDS-TUCKER AGITATION.

The enjoyment of peace was short. Days of sore trial were at hand. In the summer of 1881, a crusade was inaugurated against the Saints to suppress their institution of plural marriage. It was begun by sectarian opponents and politicians. Beginning in Utah, the agitation soon spread throughout the whole land. Alarming falsehoods of Mormon disloyalty, vice, and abominations, soon stirred the people of the nation and their national representatives to a fever heat against the Saints. The politicians were actuated by a hunger for spoils and the emoluments of office, while the ministers were evidently led by disappointment or innate hate. Neither class cared so much for polygamy as for these other considerations. Congress was pressed to enact the pending proscriptive measures. Memorials, protests, declarations, and petitions of the Mormons denying the industriously circulated falsehoods, were of no avail.

The Edmunds law, supplemental to the law of 1862, which had practically remained a dead letter, was signed by President Arthur on the 22nd of March, 1882, and became law. Polygamy was made punishable by disfranchisement, also a fine of not more than five hundred dollars and imprisonment for not more than three years. Cohabitation with more than one woman was punishable by a fine of not to exceed three hundred dollars and imprisonment not to exceed six months. Polygamists and believers in the doctrine of plural marriage were rendered incompetent to act as jurors. No polygamist could hold office, or vote. In 1887 a supplemental act was passed known as the Edmunds-Tucker law. This gave additional powers to the officers, required certificates of all marriages to be filed in the offices of the probate courts (whose judges were appointed by the President of the United States), disincorporated the Church and ordered the Supreme Court to wind up its affairs, and to take possession of its escheated property.

Twelve thousand persons were disfranchised. A test oath was subcsribed to by those Mormons who decided to retain their rights of franchise, the election machinery having been placed in the hands of a commission of five, appointed by the President of the United States. Their political rights thus interdicted, the Mormons were set upon by the judiciary. Mr. Rudger Clawson was the first to answer the charge of polygamy and unlawful cohabitation before the courts. He was found guilty and sentenced, November 3rd, 1884, to four years imprisonment and to pay a fine of $800. Then followed an unjustifiably cruel legal persecution. Upwards of a thousand men were sent to the penitentiary because they would not promise to discard their families. Hundreds were driven into retirement or exile, families were broken up. There was untold sorrow and heart-suffering in their midst. Juries obtained by open venire were unanimous in obeying the bidding of over zealous prosecuting attorneys who were determined on conviction. As a rule to be suspected was equivalent to arrest, arrest to indictment, indictment to conviction, conviction to the full penalty of the law. Unprincipled, some of them very immoral, adventurers dogged the steps or raided the homes of respectable veterans, founders of the commonwealth. Government aided in the enforcement of the law by increased special appropriations. Paid spotters and spies prowled among the people. Children were questioned about their parents' affairs; wives, daughters and maidens were often compelled to submit to the shamefully indecent questions with which professional grand juries pestered them. The Saints were passing through a night of dreary darkness. Bereft of the counsels and presence of their leaders, torn with anguish, they were taught the lessons of self-reliance, dependence upon the Lord, faith in God. As a community they never faltered, never permitted themselves to be led into acts of violence against their persecutors, though the provocations were numerous and ample. Their enemies, too, desired that they might commit some overt act that a pretext might be found for their utter destruction.

Under these circumstances, President John Taylor, who had retired from public view February 1st, 1885, died in exile, July 25th, 1887. Thus mourned by Israel in bondage, he passed away a double martyr to the cause he loved, for with him it was "The Kingdom of God or nothing." Said his counselors, in the official announcement of his death: "President John Taylor has been killed by the cruelty of officials who have, in this territory, misrepresented the Government of the United States."

---

3. CHANGED CONDITIONS.

Upon the Twelve Apostles, with Wilford Woodruff as chief, now devolved the responsibility of the presidency. Apostles Cannon and Smith took their former places in the quorum of the Twelve.

In this capacity the Apostles continued to act until the annual conference in 1889, when the First Presidency, for the fourth time, was organized, on the 7th day of April, Wilford Woodruff being chosen President. He selected George Q. Cannon and Joseph F. Smith as his counselors.

The crusade continued unabated, probably with less hardship, since the people were in a measure adjusting themselves to their trying conditions. The political history of this period was as full of acts breathing bitterness against the Mormons, as was the judicial. The executive was in full harmony with the judiciary, and their united efforts to crush the people will some day appear as little to their credit as the history of these times, once told in full, will redound to the honor of the afflicted Saints.

In the courts the Mormons contested every step taken by the Government to deprive them of what they considered their religious rights. They deemed plural marriage part of their creed and faith, hence, strongly maintained that Congress could make no law prohibiting the free exercise thereof. But the Supreme Court of the nation, before which tribunal the laws were finally tested, while condemning some of the cruel and unjust methods of enforcing the law, decided that the enactments to suppress plural marriage were constitutional, and that the first amendment to the Constitution, providing for the free exercise of religion, can not be used to defend this doctrine.

Meanwhile the Government continued unyielding in its determination to suppress the practice, having in contemplation and threatening the adoption of still harsher measures than used heretofore.

It was while the Saints were in the midst of these afflictions that President Woodruff sought the Lord in their behalf, and in answer to his petitions of anguish, received the word of the Lord authorizing him to advise the Saints to discontinue the practice of plural marriage.

A manifesto to this effect was issued on the 24th of September, 1890, and at the following semi-annual conference, October 6th, the assembled Saints accepted the declaration of their leader concerning plural marriage as authoritative and binding. Since then the doctrine has neither been taught nor practiced.

The people had done their duty. God revealed the doctrine to them; He it was who authorized its suspension. In the face of appalling opposition, they had firmly and openly defended it for thirty years. They were justified by their sacrifice and suffering. God accepted of their offerings as He had done once before, when they were hindered in the performance of His will, in Jackson County.* The design of God so far had been accomplished. In defending themselves, they had been given the privilege to explain the gospel, to bear their testimonies to the mission of so-called Mormonism, in the nation's high places, under other conditions rendered inaccessible.

Looked upon at first with some suspicion, the Government and people of the nation at length believed the Mormons sincere, as they are, in their avowal to discontinue plural marriages. This, with the change in

---

* Doctrine and Covenants, Section 124, verses 49 to 54.
Robert's Ecclesiastical History, p, 457, notes 6, 7, 8.

political affairs wrought by the disunion of their People's (Mormon) political party, and the adoption by them of National politics, by which the Saints, heretofore united in all things, have become politically divided, has brought about the present era of "good feelings and changed conditions."

The last remnant of their most bitter enemy, the local Liberal Party, having outlived its mission, is passing away to deserved oblivion.

---

4. THE TEMPLES OF THE SAINTS.

Four magnificent temples, in which the Saints are doing a noble work for the living and the dead, have been reared in Utah to the name of God—one in St. George, dedicated January 1st, 1877; one in Logan, dedicated May 17th, 1884; one in Manti, dedicated May 21st, 1888; one in Salt Lake City, dedicated April 6th, 1893. The completion and dedication of the temple in Salt Lake City have been among the most important events in the administration of President Woodruff.

At the annual conference, April 6th, 1892, the capstone was laid, the ceremonies taking place in the presence of forty thousand people—the largest assemblage ever congregated together in the history of the Church. Nearly all the leading authorities were present to swell the "Hosanna" shouts of the Saints who had come to witness the ceremonies for which they had longed and waited these many years. Services at 10 a.m. on the morning of the 6th were first held in the Tabernacle. The great audience of twelve thousand, with the many thousands who could not gain admission, adjourned to the south side of the temple at 11 a.m.

First in the march came the choir, then the First Presidency, the Apostles, followed by the other quorums of the Priesthood, in their order to the least. The ceremonies, though simple, have never been excelled for enthusiasm and impressiveness in the history of the people. After music and song, prayer having been offered by President Joseph. F. Smith, all things being in readiness, President Wilford Woodruff stepped to the front of the platform, saying: "Attention, all ye house of Israel, and all ye nations of the earth. We will now lay the topstone of the temple of our God, the foundation of which was laid and dedicated by the Prophet, Seer, and Revelator, Brigham Young." He then pressed a button, and by means of electricity the last stone of the holy structure was laid. Then followed a grand effect: forty thousand voices, led by Apostle Lorenzo Snow, shouted in concert, "Hosanna, hosanna, hosanna to God and the Lamb. Amen, amen, and amen." This was repeated three times, each shout being accompanied by a waving of handkerchiefs. A resolution was then adopted, amid cheers from the vast assembly, to complete the building so that the dedication might take place on April 6th, 1893. After a closing anthem, the benediction was pronounced by President George Q. Cannon.

With energy and determination work was now pushed with a view to complete the interior of the grand structure by the appointed time, an undertaking which seemed almost impossible in so short a period. However, the people donated liberally of their means, the best workmen were employed, and with the blessings of God upon their labors, the task was accomplished.

On Tuesday, April 4th, 1893, the annual conference began in the Tabernacle, continuing for two days. On the morning of the 6th, 2,500 people who had been provided with tickets of admission met in the large assembly room on the upper floor of the temple, having first viewed the rich and magnificent interior furnishings. All the general authorities of the Church were present—the first time for many years that the First Presidency, Twelve Apostles, Patriarch, Presiding Council of Seventies, and residing Bishopric, all had been able to meet together in an assemblage of the Saints. A select choir of three hundred voices, led by Evan Stephens, sang an anthem, after which President Woodruff offered the dedicatory prayer. This was followed by appropriate, instructive and consoling remarks from Presidents Cannon, Woodruff and Smith. The Lord will comfort Zion; the day when His rich favor will be bestowed upon her is at hand; union characterizes the Priesthood—was the burden of their speech. Fogiveness and charity were impressed upon the Saints, who were assured of a brighter day in store for them than they had ever yet experienced. The Spirit bore testimony to every soul present that God had accepted the house now dedicated to Him. Many were moved to tears of joy. The toils and sacrifices of forty years received their crowning triumph in the revelation from God to each member of the Church who attended, that He had accepted of the temple as a habitation holy to His name.

In the afternoon another congregation of the Saints convened, then followed meetings until thirty-one had been held, the average attendance of each being 2,260, making a total of 70,000 people who witnessed the dedication ceremonies. There were, besides, fifteen thousand Sunday school children, for whom special services were held, making a grand total of 85,000. Members of the Church attended from every stake of Zion, as follows: Alberta, Canada; Snowflake, St. Johns, St. Joseph, and Maricopa, Arizona; Bannock, Cassia, Malad, Bear Lake and Oneida, Idaho; San Luis, Colorado; Star Valley, Wyoming; Beaver, San Juan, St. George, Panguitch Emery, Parowan, Uintah, Millard, Morgan, Summit, Sevier, Sanpete, Cache, Wasatch, Weber, Tooele, Juab, Utah, Davis, Kanab, Salt Lake, Iosepa, and Box Elder, Utah; and Old Mexico.*

The closing session of the services were held on the afternoon of Monday, April 24th, 1893, and the temple was opened for ordinances on the day of May following.

5. CONCLUSION.

Viewing as in the foregoing the panorama of the eventful past the prosperity of the present appears marvelous in our eyes—the future lustrous with bright promise.

The Latter-day Saints are a happy, prosperous, God-fearing, virtuous people steadily increasing in numbers and good works. Thrift, cleanliness, good order, peace and sobriety, are among their characteristics. While they are not wealthy, they generally own their homes, lands and herds. God has blessed the land because of them; and for their sakes the earth has yielded in abundance.

Believers in education, they are foremost in giving their offspring the advantages of a true training. Their children are steady attendants at the public schools

---

* For a complete account of the dedication services see *Contributor*, Vol. 14, p. 243.

which are found in every city, village and hamlet where they abide. Besides the institutions of learning founded by President Young, President Woodruff, a few years ago, realizing that true education is based upon a correct theology, counseled the organization of a Church school system which has grown until nearly all the stakes have their academies; and the wards, now numbering upwards of five hundred, are gradually establishing schools adapted to the capacity of younger students.

Hundreds of young missionaries go forth yearly to all parts of the earth, and return having their minds stored with fresh thoughts, new conceptions, advanced opinions, which are assimilated by the Saints, adding new vigor and life to the community. A host of 65,000 children are being trained in the Sabbath schools over ten thousand young men are studying the principles of the gospel in the Mutual Improvement Associations; the quorums of the Priesthood are training their members for the duties of the ministry, and the practical labors of life.

The people of our own country, and of the earth, are becoming more favorable to the Saints as their virtues and designs are better understood. Witness the hearty welcome recently extended to the First Presidency, and the Tabernacle Choir, a company of over four hundred, on their way to the Columbian Exposition, also the testimony of Elders in foreign countries.

What of the future? What of the destiny of this vigorous, progressive people?

Their faith is designed for the happiness, well-being and salvation, temporal and spiritual, of all the creatures of God. It is exemplified by them in noble and practical works. Their religion has inherent elements of strength, rooted in the revealed truths of Deity, that insure its perpetuity. Mormonism is not the work of men, but is the work of God. Its doctrines have been established for a wise purpose in Him, to prepare mankind for Christ's second coming and reign on earth. In short, so-called Mormonism, broad in scope, tolerant, truth-seeking, is the gospel of Jesus Christ, and as such is destined to be the religion of the future. Its truths, built upon direct revelation from God, are constantly gaining ground, and correspond perfectly to the needs of the age.

Its own centennial close at hand, with resplendent prospects in view, the Church stands upon the threshold of a new century full of bounteous promise.

The following books and pamphlets are printed and for sale by

GEORGE Q. CANNON & SONS CO.,

SALT LAKE CITY, UTAH,

—OR—

A. H. CANNON, P. O. BOX N, OGDEN, UTAH.

BOOK OF MORMON, a record of the ancient inhabitants of America, morocco, extra gilt, $3.25; calf grain, gilt, 2.50; English roan, 1.75; roan, 1.25, cloth..$1.00

DOCTRINE AND COVENANTS, containing the revelations given to Joseph Smith for the guidance of the Church, morrocco, extra gilt, 3.25; calf grain, gilt, 2.50; English roan, 1.75; roan, 1.25; cloth,... 1.00

LATTER-DAY SAINT'S HYMN BOOK, morocco, extra gilt 1.50; calf grain, gilt, 1.25; roan, .75; cloth...... .35

VOICE OF WARNING, an introduction to the faith and doctrines of the Latter-day Saints, morocco, extra gilt, 1.65; calf grain, gilt, 1.25; leather, .50; cloth stiff covers, 35; cloth, limp covers,.............. .25

ORSON PRATT'S WORKS, a series of pamphlets on the doctrines of the gospel, a book of 314 pages, ... .75

PRICE-LIST OF MORMON PUBLICATIONS.

THE LIFE OF JOSEPH SMITH, morocco, gilt, 5.00; leather gilt, 4.00; cloth, ... 3.00

THE LIFE OF BRIGHAM YOUNG, leather, 1.00; cloth, .50; paper,................................. .25

A BRIEF HISTORY OF THE CHURCH, leather, 1.00; cloth, .50; paper,............................. .25

HAND-BOOK OF REFERENCE to the history, chronology, religion and country of the Latter-day Saints, ... .50

MORMON DOCTRINE, a plain and simple explanation of the principles of the gospel, in twelve tersely-written chapters, with appendix giving scriptural references, by Charles W. Penrose, ... .25

HISTORY OF THE MORMONS AND MANIFESTO IN REGARD TO POLYGAMY................................. .05

MR. DURANT OF SALT LAKE CITY, "THAT MORMON," by Ben E. Rich,............................. 1.25

WHY WE PRACTICE PLURAL MARRIAGE, by a Mormon wife and mother—Helen Mar Whitney, paper cover, ... .25

MORGAN'S TRACTS, Nos. 1 and 2, on the Doctrines of the Gospel, each........................... .03

THE MODERN PROPHET, evidences of the divine mission of Joseph Smith,.................... .03

SPENCER'S LETTERS, exhibiting the most prominent doctrines of the Latter-day Saints, morocco, gilt $2.25; calf grain, gilt, $1.60; roan, $1.25; cloh.. 1.00

HISTORICAL AND DESCRIPTIVE SKETCH OF THE SALT LAKE TEMPLE, including the dedicatory prayer... .10

www.ingramcontent.com/pod-product-compliance
Lightning Source LLC
Chambersburg PA
CBHW020258170426
43202CB00008B/424